Arttitude

POSTER**SPY**
ALTERNATIVE
MOVIE POSTER COLLECTION

Frédéric Claquin   Jack Woodhams

Schiffer Publishing Ltd

4880 Lower Valley Road • Atglen, PA 19310

CONTENTS

INTRODUCTION

FRÉDÉRIC CLAQUIN
www.therealarttitude.com

Creating a book exclusively focused on movie posters is an idea I have had for quite some time now. For me and those who grew up in the '70s, '80s, or even early '90s, graphic design and drawing has always been an important form of communication. It should be remembered that way before the advent of YouTube, or social networks in general, the first contact you had with a movie, album, book, or video game was its cover. It was supposed to capture the essence of the world you were invited to by the artist or the director. Who hasn't been taken away by a poster by Drew Struzan? Who hasn't wanted to discover the music hidden behind a Derek Riggs album cover? And who hasn't wanted to further explore the strange world of *Dune* painted by John Schoenherr?

Now, marketing campaigns give us a flood of images and photos, a process that might as well be hard selling. This book pays tribute to the era of cinematographic works that made us dream. This project is also the first collaboration with Jack Woodhams' PosterSpy, one of the most influential websites devoted to alternative posters. This collaboration with PosterSpy is the first of a series that promises to be fantastic!

INTRODUCTION

JACK WOODHAMS
www.posterspy.com

Illustrated posters were a huge part of the movie industry as early as the 1930s and probably earlier. In the '70s and '80s, artists like Drew Struzan, John Alvin, Bob Peak, Saul Bass, and Richard Amsel created some of the most famous and iconic movie posters from their time. Sadly, we don't see this style used that often in modern movie marketing.

Recently, artists have started creating posters for their favorite movies and it has become a huge movement. I recommend anyone reading this book to watch *24x36: A Movie about Movie Posters* directed by Kevin Burke. The film details the fascinating progression of movie posters over time. This book is a celebration of talent, art, creativity, and the love for movies that holds the alternative poster movement together.

Back in 2013, I set up PosterSpy as a blog and I shared some of my favorite alternative poster designs. As a film fan and creative myself, it felt like a great way to express my love for pop culture while showcasing incredible art I was finding online. In 2014, the PosterSpy website launched—a showcase platform for alternative poster artists. I figured it would be great to have a website where anyone can access thousands of posters created by artists. Now in 2018, hundreds of artists from around the world have uploaded more than 10,000 posters. Still to this day, I'm not quite sure how the website grew like it did, it's truly incredible and I'm very thankful to all the artists supporting the platform.

This book is a collection of some of the best artwork from our website. Originally planned as an e-book, I soon realized that the love for art books comes from their form, and such amazing art deserves to be presented in a more beautiful way than on a screen.

Included are fifty-eight artists featured across more than 200 pages of artwork. I'm incredibly proud and thankful that I'm able to present it to you.

MICHAEL SHANNON
JOEL EDGERTON
KIRSTEN DUNST
ADAM DRIVER
SAM SHEPARD
A FILM BY JEFF NICHOLS
MIDNIGHT SPECIAL
HOUSTON, TEXAS
29.7604° N, 95.3698° W
LIVINGSTON,MONTANA
47.0000° N, 110.0000° W
ATLANTA, GA
33.7550° N, 84.3900° W
SAN ANGELO
CHARLOTTE, NORTH CAROLINA
35.2269° N, 80.8433° W
HE'S NOT LIKE US

ADAM COCKERTON
www.posterspy.com/profile/adamcockerton

Although I've been an art director working for the entertainment industry for over a decade, I'm a relative newcomer to illustration. I couldn't tell you why, I just know I need to draw more; it fills a gap in the creative process that is often overlooked with client work.

I've had a passion for the illustrated poster for longer than I can remember. The cinema in my local town used to keep quads stacked up in a locked cupboard. As a 10-year-old I used to find a way in through an open window and "borrow" them! I'd collected some of the finest movie poster art I could get my hands on, much later on I'd find out I had art by my design heroes Bob Peak and Drew Struzan, and, boom, I was hooked. Who says nothing comes of a misspent youth?

I am really grateful to be part of the PosterSpy book and join the global underground movement to create alternatives to studio campaign material, especially appearing among so many illustrators much more experienced than myself.

I am Adam Cockerton, I live in London, and I am a posterholic!

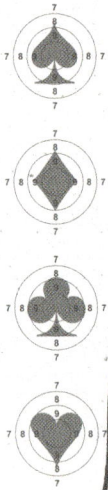

宮崎駿監督作品

千と千尋の神隠し

MIYAZAKI'S

SPIRITED AWAY

TOHO PRESENTS A STUDIO GHIBLI FILM

RUMI HIIRAGI · MIYU IRINO · MARI NATSUKI WITH BUNTA SUGAWARA · "SPIRITED AWAY"
EDITED BY TAKESHI SEYAMA MUSIC BY JOE HISAISHI CINEMATOGRAPHY BY ATSUSHI OKUI
PRODUCED BY TOSHIO SUZUKI WRITTEN BY HAYAO MIYAZAKI
DIRECTED BY HAYAO MIYAZAKI

WILLIAM FOX
PRESENTS

SUNRISE

A
SONG
OF
TWO
HUMANS

GEORGE O'BRIEN ◆ JANET GAYNOR
SCENARIO BY CARL MAYER ◆ FROM AN ORIGINAL THEME BY HERMANN SUDERMANN
PHOTOGRAPHY BY CHARLES ROSHER & KARL STRAUSS
DIRECTED BY F.W. MURNAU

ADAM MCDANIEL
www.adammcdaniel.com
www.posterspy.com/profile/adammcdaniel

Movies and art have given me many treasured memories. They've inspired my dreams and career path, and even helped me through hard times.

A child in the 1980s, I lived, breathed, and loved movies. But however great my experiences then—this was, after all, the decade of *Indiana Jones*, decent *Star Wars* sequels, *Back to the Future*, and a pre-nippled Batman—I think what excited me most, whenever stepping beneath that local town center theater marquee, was the chance to see the latest round of movie posters.

When I say "movie poster," I'm not referring to the cookie-cutter, Photoshop templates that have become the norm these days. I'm talking about real movie posters, the big, artful, sometimes cheesy, often delightful product

of some guy who actually sat down behind a drafting table, put pencil to paper, and created magic. It's probably the toughest art to master for any illustrator. Richard Amsel, Bob Peak, Drew Struzan—those guys are giants to me. Their work builds upon the anticipation, the promise, and the excitement of what (hopefully) is in store when we go into the theater.

Adam McDaniel is an award-winning artist, filmmaker, and writer. His artwork has been profiled in the feature documentaries 24x36 and Indyfans, *and published by Intrada Music, Tantrum Books, and the Newport Beach Film Festival, among others. He currently works at Warner Bros., and is filming a feature documentary on the late illustrator, Richard Amsel (Raiders of the Lost Ark).*

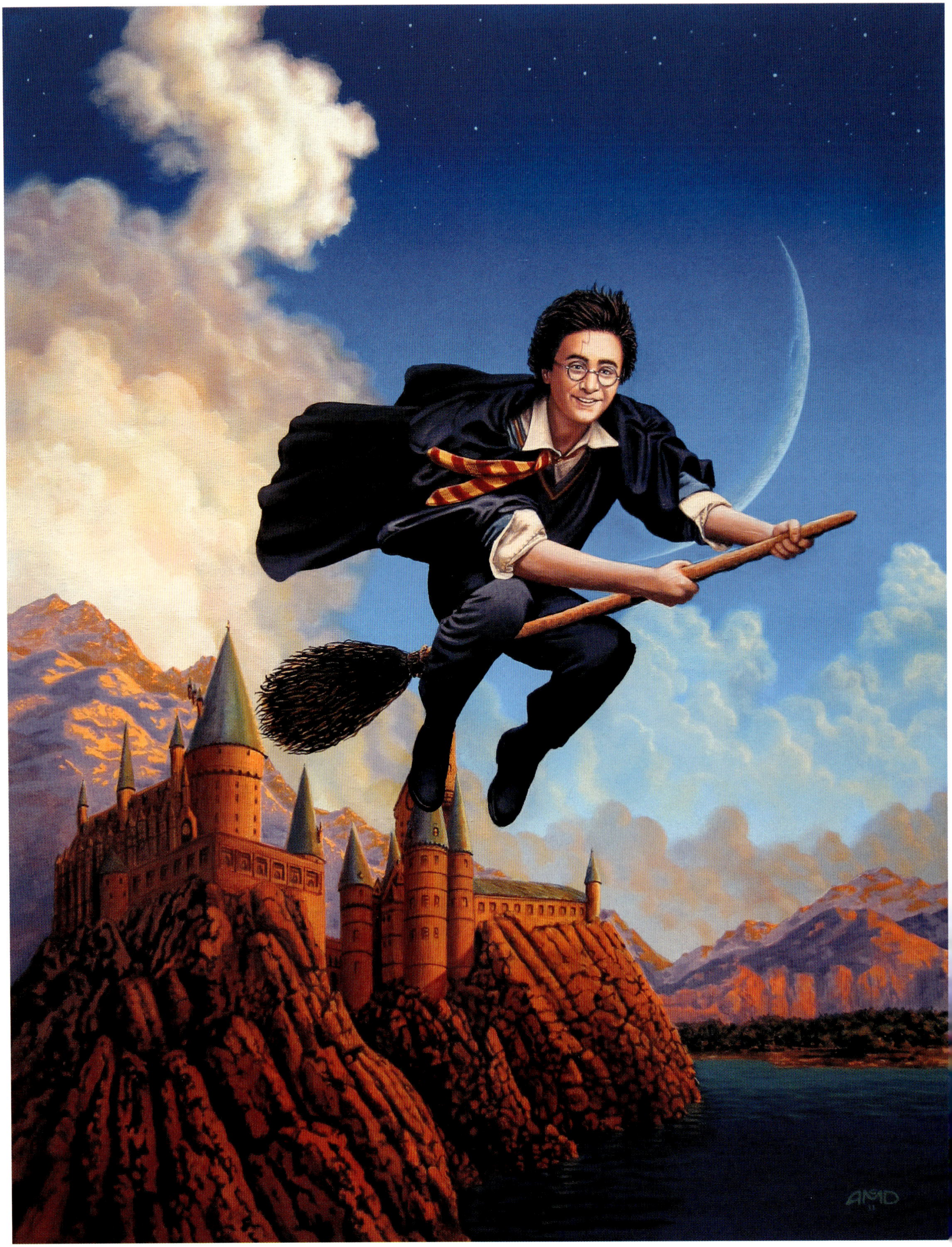

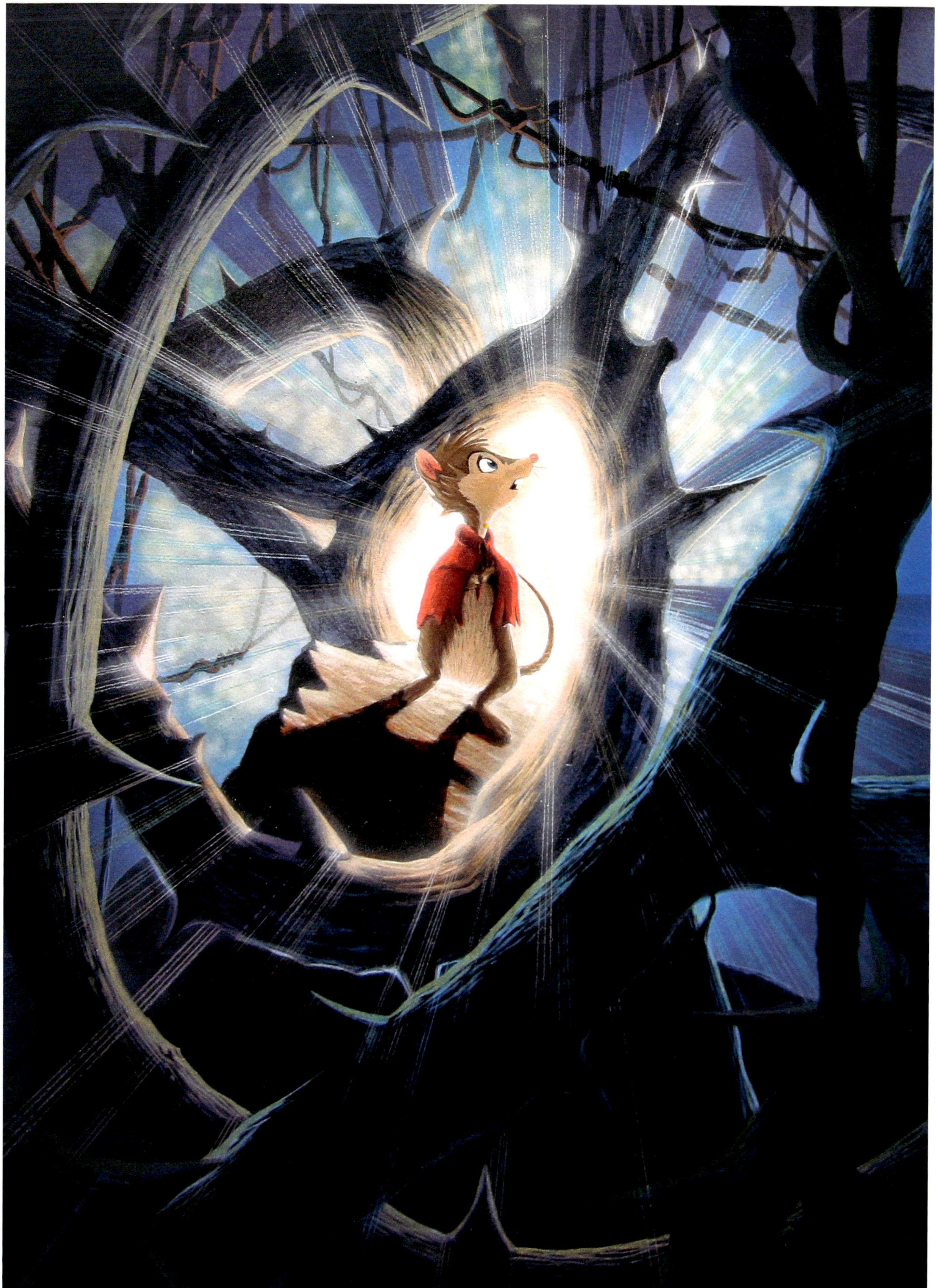

The Addams Family

PARAMOUNT PICTURES PRESENTS A SCOTT RUDIN PRODUCTION A BARRY SONNENFELD FILM
ANJELICA HUSTON RAUL JULIA CHRISTOPHER LLOYD CHRISTINA RICCI JIMMY WORKMAN
DAN HEDAYA ELIZABETH WILSON JUDITH MALINA CAREL STRUYCKEN DANA IVEY
WRITTEN BY CAROLINE THOMPSON & LARRY WILSON CHARACTERS CREATED BY CHARLES ADDAMS MUSIC MARC SHAIMAN
CINEMATOGRAPHY BY OWEN ROIZMAN FILM EDITING BY DEDE ALLEN & JIM MILLER ASSOCIATE PRODUCERS BONNIE ARNOLD & PAUL ROSENBERG
CO-PRODUCER JACK CUMMINS EXECUTIVE PRODUCER GRAHAM PLACE PRODUCED BY SCOTT RUDIN DIRECTED BY BARRY SONNENFELD

ANDREW SWAINSON
www.andrewswainson.com
www.posterspy.com/profile/andrew-swainson

The first time I became aware of film posters was when I was about six or seven years old on a trip to our local cinema. As we queued to go in, there was a poster advertising what was showing the following week and it left a very vivid stain on my memory. A white background, a bold black triangle, a sinister face under a bowler hat, false lashes on one eye, a clenched fist gripping a short dagger thrusting out of the frame and on his sleeve a cuff link formed from a single eyeball. It was of course Philip Castle's poster for Kubrick's *A Clockwork Orange*. It was mesmerising (and quite frightening) . . . what was THAT film about? So I grew up loving films and the art that was used to promote them. I've spent my professional life as a graphic

designer and (very) occasional illustrator but the alternative film poster world had entirely escaped my attention until I randomly stumbled upon Ken Taylor's *20,000 Leagues Under the Sea* in 2012. At first I thought it was an old poster, but after a little investigation I uncovered this whole scene and the online communities that followed it. It was like taking the red pill in *The Matrix*. After summoning up the courage to put some work out myself, it has gone from being a hobby that got out of hand to being part of my working life. It has also introduced me to a lot of new friends around the world, the support of whom has been a great help over the last few years. It means a lot to me.

TWENTIETH CENTURY FOX PRESENTS A BRANDYWINE PRODUCTION

A L I E N

TOM SKERRITT   SIGOURNEY WEAVER   VERONICA CARTWRIGHT   HARRY DEAN STANTON
JOHN HURT   IAN HOLM   YAPHET KOTTO

Executive Producer   Produced by   Directed by
RONALD SHUSETT   GORDON CARROLL, DAVID GILER and WALTER HILL   RIDLEY SCOTT

Story by   Screenplay by   Music by
DAN O'BANNON and RONALD SHUSETT   DAN O'BANNON   JERRY GOLDSMITH

A HAMMER FILM PRODUCTION

DRACULA

PETER CUSHING, MICHEAL GOUGH, MELISSA STRIBLING and CHRISTOPHER LEE as Dracula

Written by JIMMY SANGSTER   Associate Producer ANTHONY NELSON KEYS

Produced by ANTHONY HINDS   Directed by TERENCE FISHER   Executive Producer MICHAEL CARRERAS

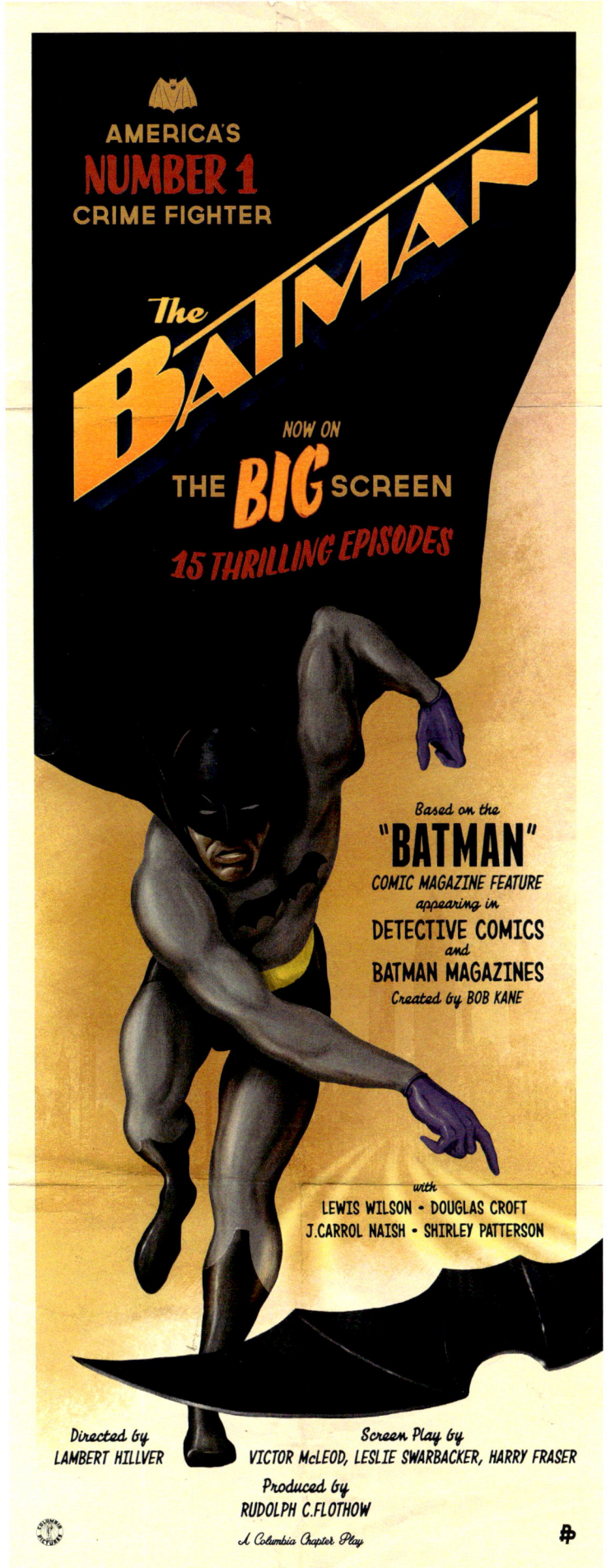

The Big Lebowski

JEFF BRIDGES JOHN GOODMAN STEVE BUSCEMI JULIANNE MOORE JOHN TURTURRO SAM ELLIOTT

The
BIG LEBOWSKI

DAVID HUDDLESTON PHILIP SEYMOUR HOFFMAN BEN GAZZARA PETER STORMARE FLEA TORSTEN VOGES TARA REID DAVID THEWLIS

AMERICA'S
NUMBER 1
CRIME FIGHTER

The
BATMAN

NOW ON
THE BIG SCREEN
15 THRILLING EPISODES

Based on the
"BATMAN"
COMIC MAGAZINE FEATURE
appearing in
DETECTIVE COMICS
and
BATMAN MAGAZINES
Created by BOB KANE

with
LEWIS WILSON · DOUGLAS CROFT
J. CARROL NAISH · SHIRLEY PATTERSON

Directed by
LAMBERT HILLYER

Screen Play by
VICTOR McLEOD, LESLIE SWABACKER, HARRY FRASER

Produced by
RUDOLPH C. FLOTHOW

A Columbia Chapter Play

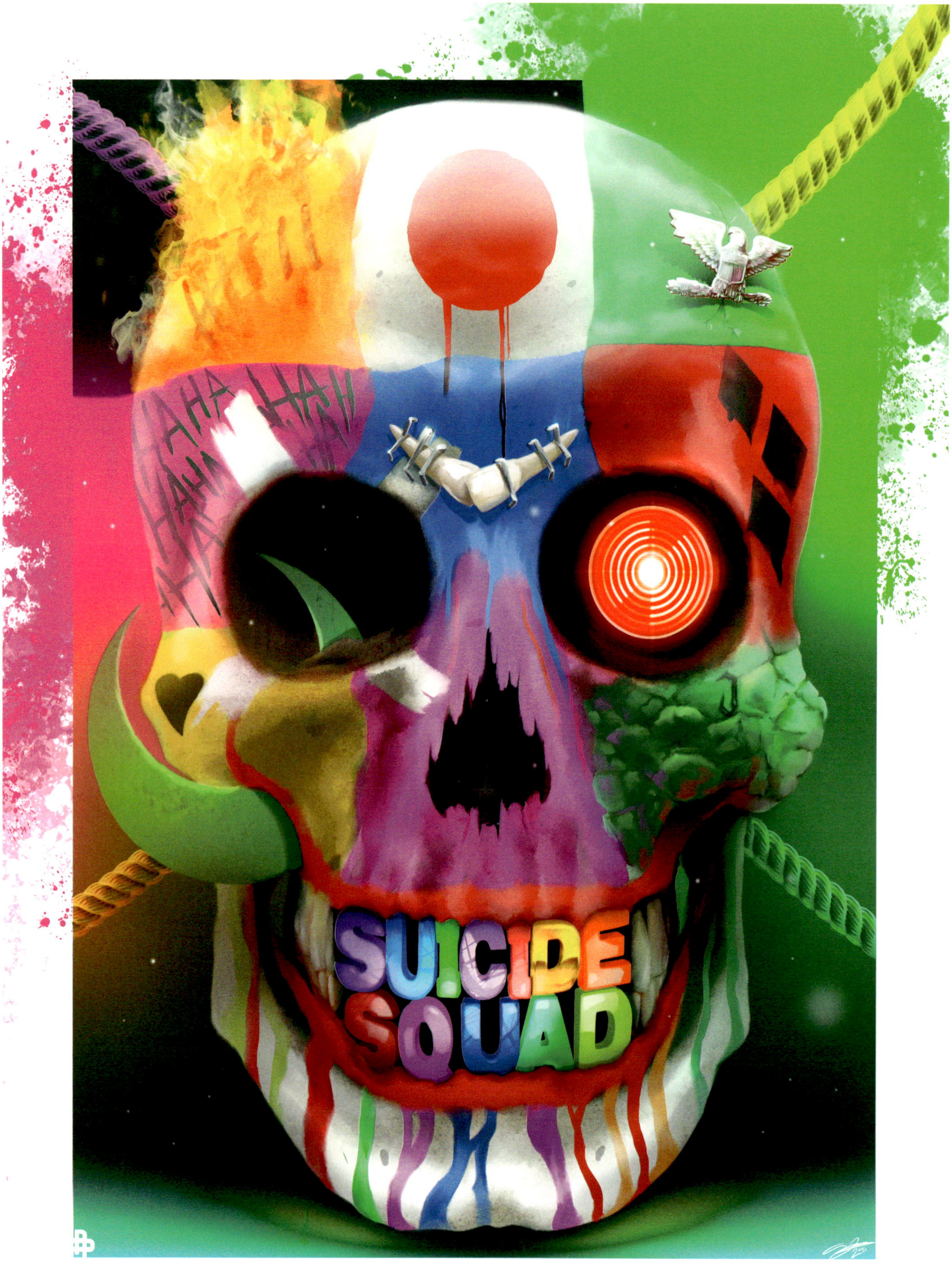
HA HA HA
SUICIDE SQUAD

ANDY FAIRHURST

www.andyfairhurstart.com
www.posterspy.com/profile/andyfairhurst/

I have always been an artist, but for my poster and pop culture art, it really has opened up a new lease on life for me in the last few years. I love the play on words (or imagery in my case) you can get away with in posters. Coming up with new ideas is always half of the fun of doing them. I've had the good fortune to work for such clients as Lucasfilm, Disney, the BBC, and 20th Century Fox. My work has been exhibited at Bottleneck Gallery (New York), Hero Complex Gallery (Los Angeles), and iam8bit (Los Angeles). I'm also a member of a great collective of artists called the Poster Posse, which is where this all started for me.

GOONIES NEVER SAY DIE

BabyRuth

SWENSENS

Steven Spielberg Presents

THE GOONIES

A RICHARD DONNER FILM "THE GOONIES" STORY BY STEVEN SPIELBERG SCREENPLAY BY CHRIS COLUMBUS
STARRING SEAN ASTIN JOSH BROLIN JEFF COHEN COREY FELDMAN KERRI GREEN MARTHA PLIMPTON JONATHAN KE QUAN
MUSIC BY DAVE GRUSIN EXECUTIVE PRODUCERS STEVEN SPIELBERG FRANK MARSHALL KATHLEEN KENNEDY
PRODUCED BY RICHARD DONNER & STEVEN SPIELBERG DIRECTED BY RICHARD DONNER

PG PARENTAL GUIDANCE SUGGESTED
SOME MATERIAL MAY NOT BE SUITABLE FOR CHILDREN

DOLBY STEREO

AMBLIN
ENTERTAINMENT

WB

ANNE BANCROFT — DUSTIN HOFFMAN — KATHERINE ROSS

THE GRADUATE

JOSEPH E. LEVINE PRESENTS
A MIKE NICHOLS — LAWRENCE TURMAN PRODUCTION
SCREENPLAY BY CALDER WILLINGHAM AND BUCK HENRY
SONGS BY PAUL SIMON PERFORMED BY SIMON AND GARFUNKEL
PRODUCED BY LAWRENCE TURMAN DIRECTED BY MIKE NICHOLS

ARDEN AVETT
www.cargocollective.com/ardenavett
www.posterspy.com/profile/arden-avett

A film poster, when it is well-made, is for me something which can be successfully described with the word "art." Furthermore, a poster is for me the medium which is best suited for conveying impressions and experiences associated with the perception of the film. In my opinion, a poster should create emotions in the viewer, it should cause a person to stop.

I always create my works with one rule in mind, which I like to define as "single image—whole story," as long as it's not a commercial project for a big brand where it needs another solution. By using a single, simple frame, I try to tell the most important thing from the film, the story presented in it. The images describing what is going on are not always clear at first glance. I'm talking about a game with the viewer: will he be able to guess the meaning of the film through a bold image? The most important thing for me is for my poster to describe what I think and how I see the film.

SIEDMIU
WSPANIAŁYCH
THE MIRISCH COMPANY
MIRISCH — ALPHA
"SIEDMIU WSPANIAŁYCH"
YUL BRYNNER • ELI WALLACH • STEVE McQUEEN
CHARLES BRONSON • ROBERT VAUGHN HORST BUCHHOLZ
WALTER MIRISCH WILLIAM ROBERTS
JOHN STURGES

LET'S MAKE AMERICA GREAT AGAIN
THE
PURGE
ELECTION YEAR
HAVE YOUR SAY JULY 4TH
WWW.THEPURGEELECTIONYEAR.COM

Emanuelle in Black Emanuelle
X
with Karin Schubert
also starring Angelo Infanti · Don Powell · Isabelle Marchal · Venantino Venantini
and with Gabriele Tinti · Music by Nico Fidenco · Directed by Albert Thomas

LE PARFUM
HISTOIRE D'UN MEURTRIER

Ben Whishaw · Alan Rickman · Rachel Hurd-Wood et Dustin Hoffman
dans "Le Parfum — Histoire d'un Meurtrier" PERFUME — A STORY OF A MURDERER · d'après le roman de Patrick Süskind
scénario de Andrew Birkin & Bernd Eichinger & Tom Tykwer musique de Tom Tykwer director de la photographie Frank Grieb
produit par Bernd Eichinger réalisé par Tom Tykwer

FLASH GORDON

BEN TURNER
www.etsy.com/shop/BenTurnerDesigns
www.posterspy.com/profile/bturnerinfo

Being a kid from the '80s, the movie posters hanging in cinema lobbies were generally the first introduction to upcoming films. No internet, no easy access to trailers, except those before the feature presentation (which seemed so fleeting in the darkened cinema anyway). You couldn't pore over every detail like you can today. But you could with the posters. The posters would always be there, staring back at me, feeding my imagination. With the illustration work, it has always been my desire to recreate that sense of wonder and anticipation that I feel when seeing a great piece of film art. It has always been my goal to intrigue people, to draw them to a film that they may not have seen or heard of before. There's also that desire to capture an image, a moment, or an idea that maybe hadn't been portrayed or thought of yet with a particular film. I strive to discover that different angle that's going to set it apart. There may be a lot more platforms out there now, but a beautifully designed poster can be so evocative, it will get me every time.

ARMY of DARKNESS

GALAXY QUEST

WET HOT AMERICAN SUMMER

AMERICAN PSYCHO

AMERICAN PSYCHO

31
ROB ZOMBIE PRESENTS 31 SHERI MOON ZOMBIE LEW TEMPLE
RICHARD BRAKE ELIZABETH DAILY MALCOLM MCDOWELL AND MEG FOSTER
WRITTEN BY ROB ZOMBIE DIRECTED BY ROB ZOMBIE DIRECTOR OF GRAPHICS

CHRIS GAROFALO
www.quiltfacestudios.storenvy.com
www.posterspy.com/profile/QFSChris

Any movie poster that both conceptually and visually commands me to see the movie it's representing is always a real treat. I've checked out so many films based entirely on the poster art, and I've been impressed more times than disappointed. As a poster artist, finding that concept that embodies the film without giving it away is as challenging as it is rewarding. That formula is a total influence on my design work. A great concept is the best way to engage the audience and generate interest, plus it's the most fun approach to take. I always try to capture the vibe of the movie subject at hand, something that die hard fans will relate to and brand new fans will be intrigued by.

the town that
dreaded sundown

THE COLONIAL THEATRE PRESENTS THE TOWN THAT DREADED SUNDOWN
10.07.2016 BEN JOHNSON ANDREW PRINE DAWN WELLS CINDY BUTLER AND BUD DAVIS
EXECUTIVE PRODUCER SAMUEL Z. ARKOFF WRITTEN BY EARL E. SMITH DIRECTED BY CHARLES B. PIERCE

36

THE
LOST · BOYS
WARNER BROS. PRESENTS A RICHARD DONNER PRODUCTION A JOEL SCHUMACHER FILM
“THE LOST BOYS” COREY FIELDMAN JAMI GERTZ COREY HAIM EDWARD HERRMANN
BARNAD HUGHES JASON PATRIC KIEFER SUTHERLAND AND DIANNE WIEST
MUSIC BY THOMAS NEWMAN EDITED BY ROBERT BROWN DIRECTOR OF PHOTOGRAPHY MICHAEL CHAPMAN
EXECUTIVE PRODUCER RICHARD DONNER STORY BY JANICE FISCHER & JAMES JEREMIAS
SCREENPLAY BY JANICE FISCHER & JAMES JEREMIAS AND JEFFREY BOAM
PRODUCED BY HARVEY BERNHARD DIRECTED BY JOEL SCHUMACHER
R RESTRICTED
PANAVISION
Cranio Dsgn
DOLBY DIGITAL

Cranio Dsgn

CRANIODSGN
www.craniodsgn.es
www.posterspy.com/profile/craniodsgn

I like to make these types of posters, firstly because I am a fan of movies, and secondly because of the nostalgia. I remember in the past many movies were presented with illustrated posters, and from there arises my passion for this type of composition and design.

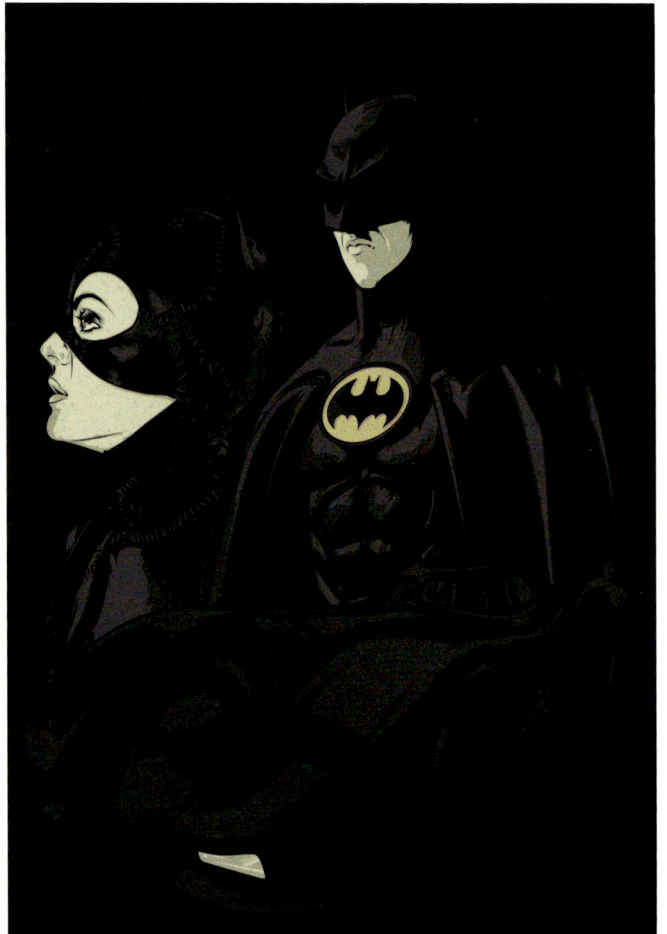

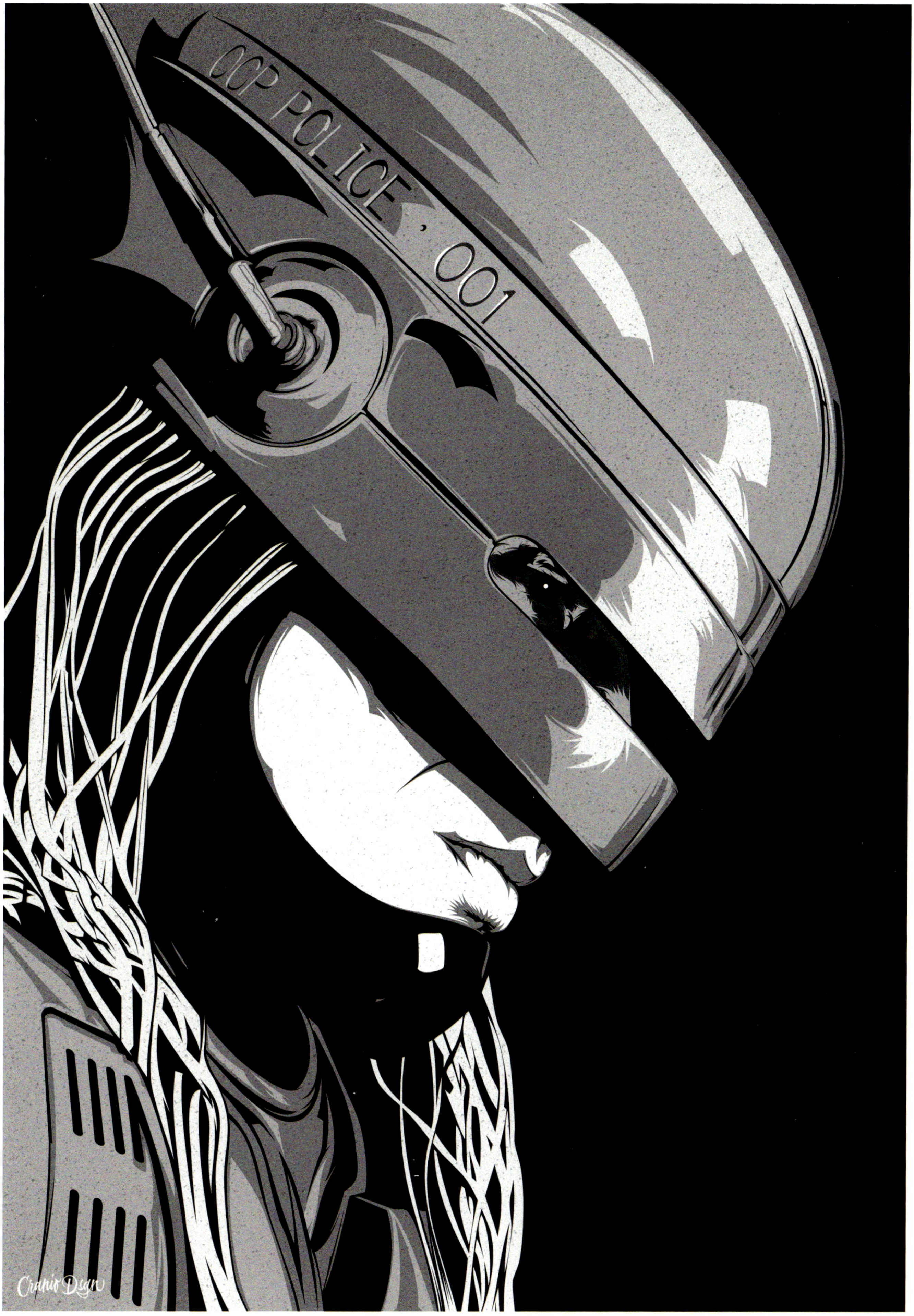
OCP POLICE · 001
Cranio Dsgn

THE GOONIES

STORY BY STEVEN SPIELBERG SCREENPLAY BY CHRIS COLUMBUS MUSIC BY DAVE GRUSIN
EXECUTIVE PRODUCERS STEVEN SPIELBERG, FRANK MARSHALL AND KATHLEEN KENNEDY
PRODUCED BY RICHARD DONNER AND HARVEY BERNHARD
DIRECTED BY RICHARD DONNER

DAN NORRIS

DAN K NORRIS
www.danielnorris.tumblr.com
www.posterspy.com/profile/danknorris

I enjoy the challenge of visual storytelling, aiming to produce work that grabs the attention and lives in the memory. Ideas should always come first, so I search for a visual hook, recombining key elements to leave the viewer feeling like they have interacted with the piece by sharing a moment of discovery. Ideas first—conflate to create.

A DAVID FINCHER FILM

FIGHT CLUB

STARRING BRAD PITT, EDWARD NORTON
AND HELENA BONHAM CARTER

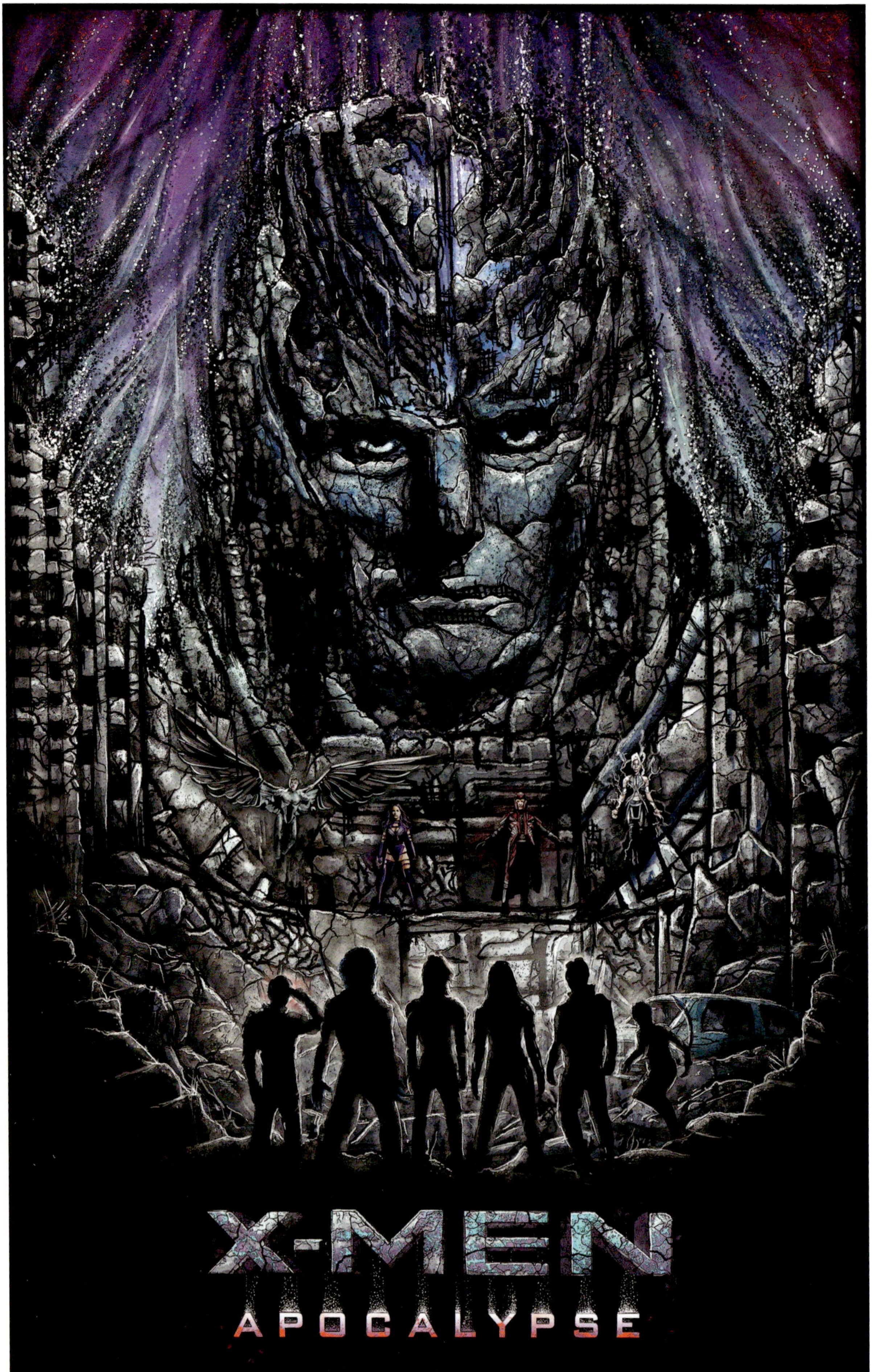
X-MEN
APOCALYPSE

DANIEL NASH
www.danielnashillustration.com
www.posterspy.com/profile/daniel-nash

I always liked the retro travel posters growing up and have been interested in pop culture and "geek" art more since I left school. It seemed to be a more accessible field to create in and get feedback from, so I guess that's what led me to want to recreate my own movie posters! I think the diverse application required is also what draws me to it, be it typographical skills or refined painting, it really keeps you on your toes as an artist.

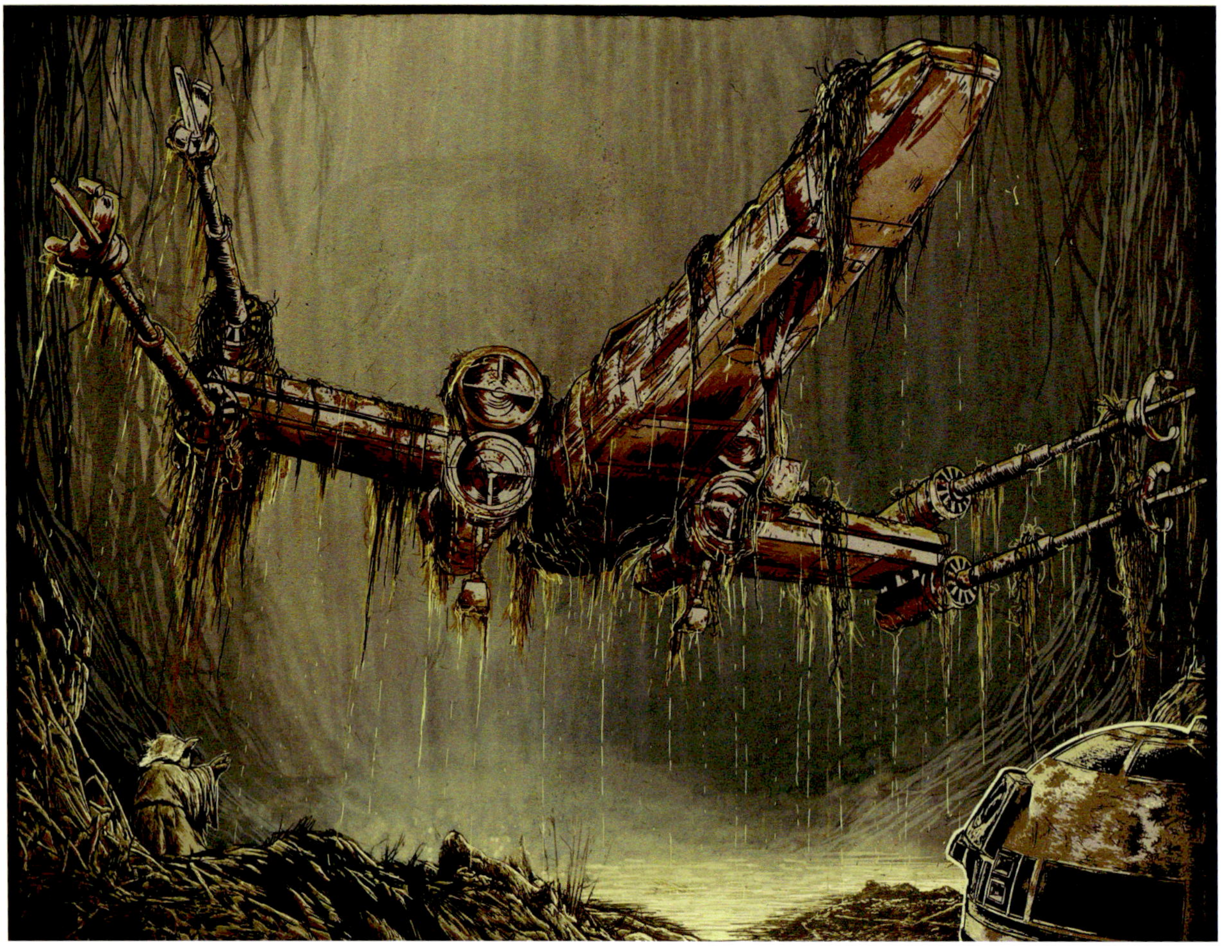

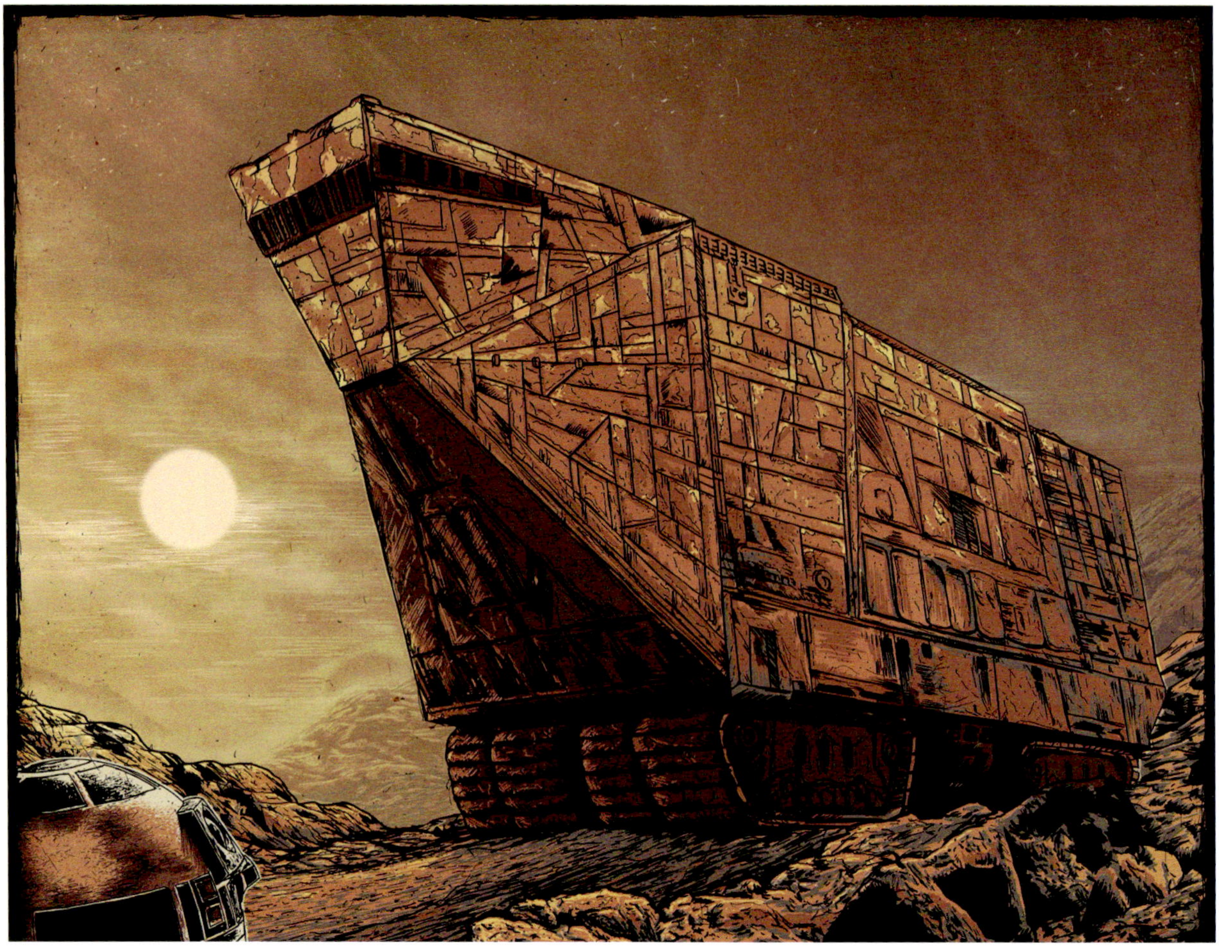

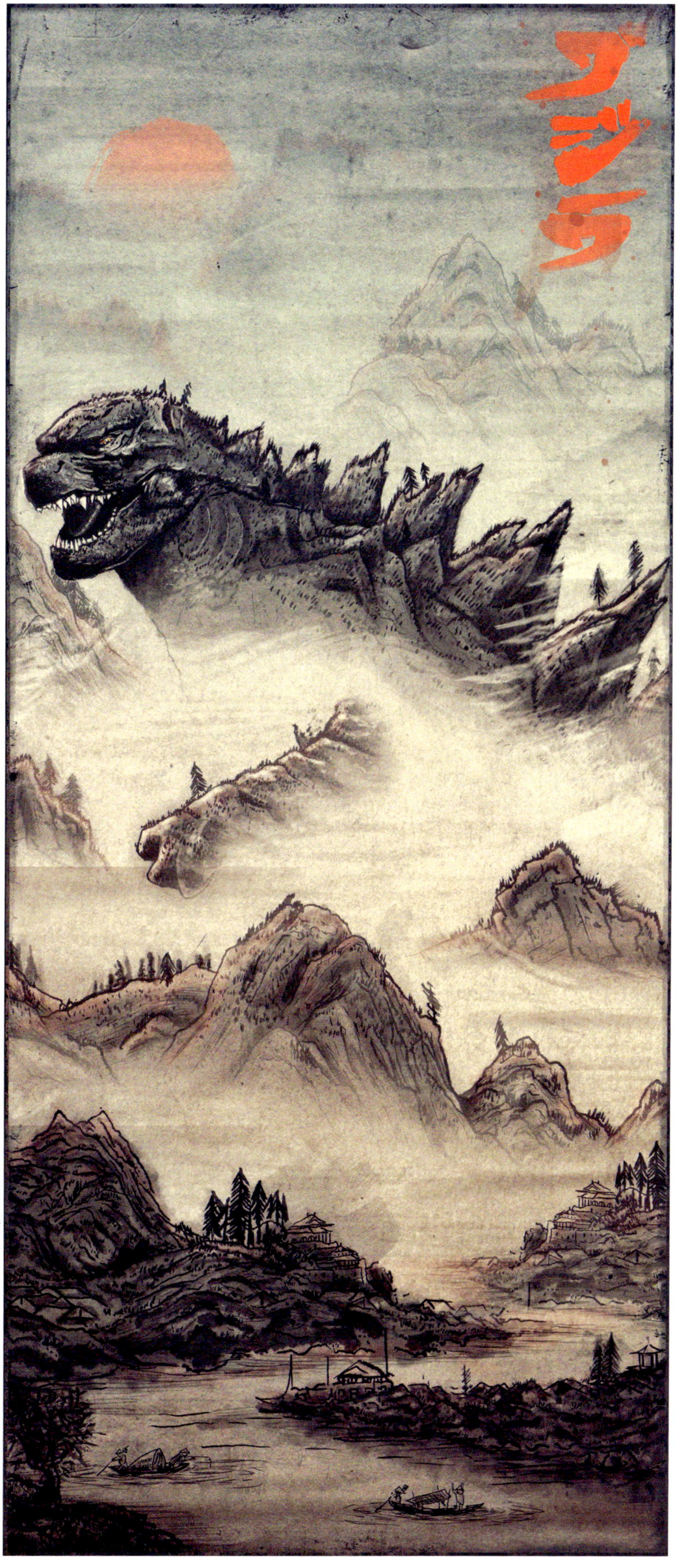
ゴジラ

VIDEODROME

A FILM BY DAVID CRONENBERG

PIERRE DAVID and VICTOR SOLNICKI Present a DAVID CRONENBERG Film ""VIDEODROME starring JAMES WOODS SONJA SMITS and DEBORAH HARRY as NICKI Also Starring PETER DVORSKY LES CARLSON
JACK CRELEY LYNNE GORMAN Special Makeup RICK BAKER Music by HOWARD SHORE Associate Producer LAWRENCE NESIS Producer CLAUDE HEROUX Executive Producer VICTOR SOLNICKI and VICTOR SOLNICKI Written and Directed by DAVID CRONENBERG
A FILMPLAN INTERNATIONAL 11 Production A UNIVERSAL Release Read the Zebra Book.
PRODUCED WITH THE PARTICIPATION OF THE CANADIAN FILM DEVELOPMENT CORPORATION AND FAMOUS PLAYERS LIMITED 1982 UNIVERSAL CITY STUDIOS, INC

DAVE

DAVE STAFFORD
www.davestafford.net
www.posterspy.com/profile/dave-stafford

From an early age, the art of movie posters had always fascinated me. The artwork is what initially draws you into that movie, and plays a vital role in the overall perception of the film. The alternative movie poster scene has given me the opportunity to give back to the lost art of movie poster design. My love of film and my love of art are combined together in my projects to create something that is not only visually appealing but also adds to a community of film enthusiasts such as those who are a part of PosterSpy.

A STANLEY KUBRICK FILM

EYES WIDE SHUT

THE SHINING

BEAUTY IS VICIOUS

A FILM BY NICOLAS WINDING REFN

THE NEON DEMON

THE ULTIMATE TRIP.

2001: A SPACE ODYSSEY

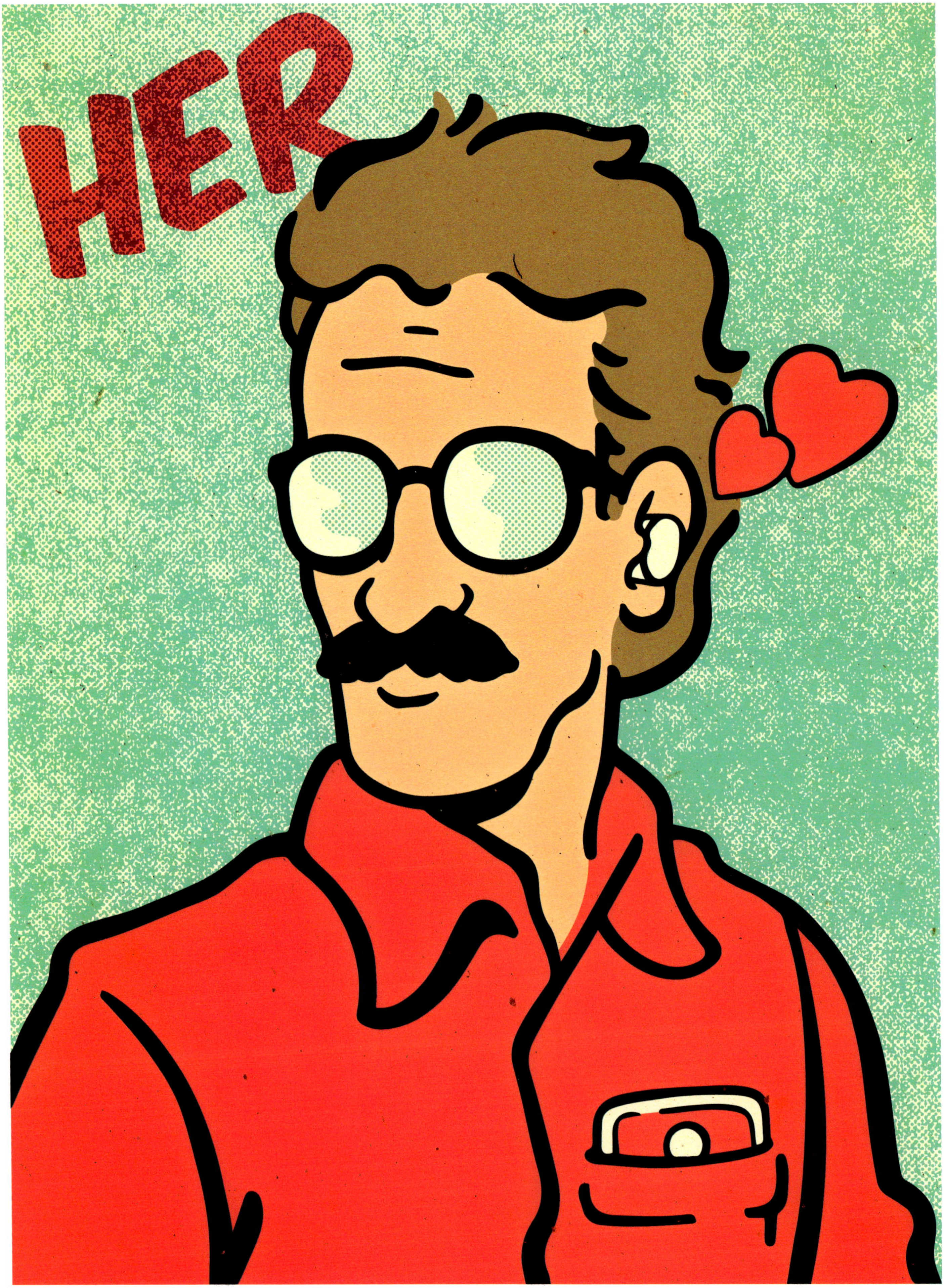
HER

DEREK EADS
www.derekeads.tumblr.com
www.posterspy.com/profile/derek-eads

I've always been drawn to movie posters because they have to sell you on a story, using one image, without spoiling anything. Before I became an artist I worked at a movie theater. One of my jobs was setting up the displays and posters for new films. I'd get to see new poster art each week and there would always be a handful of posters that really stood out and stayed with you. I think that's where my passion for poster art started.

With posters, each individual artist can bring their own take to the film and showcase the imagery they connect with the most. Others are able to look at the movie in a different way and maybe pick up on something they missed before. I love how different each poster composition can be—whether it's a grand image featuring several characters and elements, or a single object that perfectly symbolizes the film.

Movie posters have had a huge influence on my own work. I enjoy telling a piece of a story and leaving the rest open to the viewer.

STRIPES

Blades of Glory

IT GETS THE PEOPLE GOING

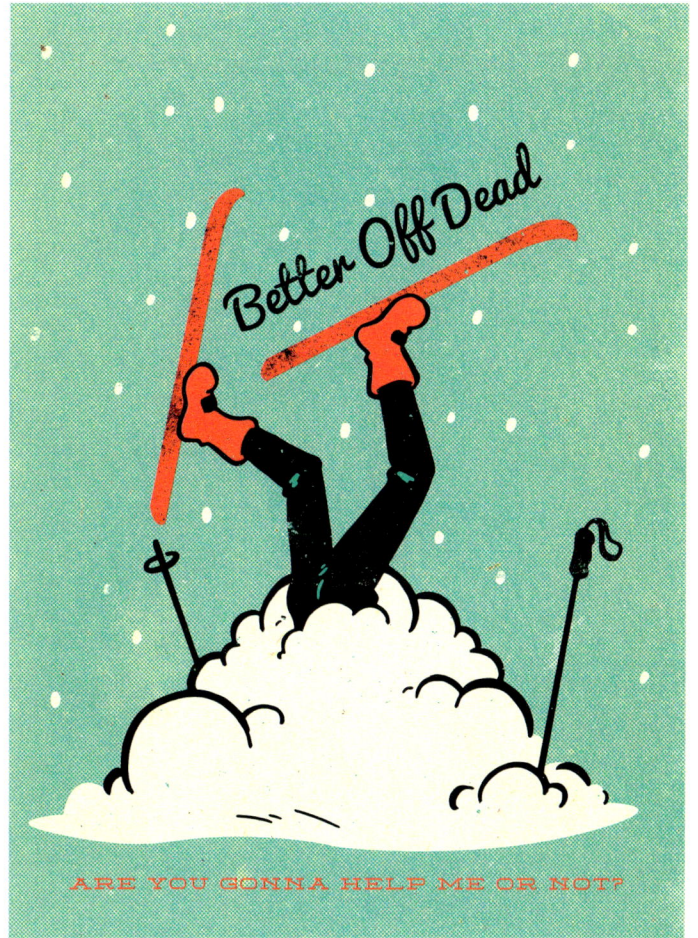

THE HOBBIT
THE DESOLATION OF SMAUG

Better Off Dead

ARE YOU GONNA HELP ME OR NOT?

Slap Shot

CAPTAIN PHILLIPS

Seven gunmen in the old
west gradually come
together to help a poor
village against savage
thieves.

DENZEL
WASHINGTON

CHRIS
PRATT

ETHAN
HAWKE

VINCENT
D'ONOFRIO

BYUNG-HUN
LEE

MANUEL
GARCIA-RULFO

MARTIN
SENSMEIR

Are the

MAGNIFICENT
SEVEN

Justice has a number

METRO-GOLDWYN-MAYER PICTURES AND COLUMBIA PICTURES PRESENT IN ASSOCIATION WITH LSTAR CAPITAL AND VILLAGE ROADSHOW PICTURES A PIN HIGH/ESCAPE ARTISTS PRODUCTION
A FILM BY ANTOINE FUQUA 'THE MAGNIFICENT SEVEN' PETER SARSGAARD MUSIC BY JAMES HORNER AND SIMON FRANGLEN COSTUME DESIGNER SHAREN DAVIS FILM EDITOR JOHN REFOUA, ACE PRODUCTION DESIGNER DEREK R. HILL
DIRECTOR OF PHOTOGRAPHY MAURO FIORE, ASC EXECUTIVE PRODUCERS WALTER MIRISCH ANTOINE FUQUA BRUCE BERMAN BEN WAISBREN SCREENPLAY BY NIC PIZZOLATTO AND RICHARD WENK PRODUCED BY ROGER BIRNBAUM TODD BLACK
MGM   VILLAGE ROADSHOW PICTURES   PG-13   Soundtrack on Sony Classical   DIRECTED BY ANTOINE FUQUA   #M897   COLUMBIA PICTURES

DOALY
www.doaly.com
www.posterspy.com/profile/doaly

I fell in love with movie posters at an early age when my parents had a video store. What I looked forward to the most was when we would have a new delivery of posters, most of the posters ended up on my bedroom wall and I would spend most nights looking at the detail on the posters, examining every brushstroke and imaging what the story could be as I was too young to watch them myself. This love of storytelling has manifested itself into my work. I love a poster that can tell a little tale or evoke an emotion about the film. It's this that gets me excited to work on a new piece because I want to delve deep and find a new way of retelling a story.

BATMAN™

BORN OF BLOOD

DOCTOR STRANGE

MARVEL

GUARDIANS OF THE GALAXY

STAR WARS

DRES13 / ANDRÉ GREPPI
www.DRES13.com
www.posterspy.com/profile/dres13

As a creative working in the advertising industry, there's a lot I could say about what I think makes film posters so great. Many times (especially before you could watch a trailer on your smartphone), the movie poster is a person's initial introduction to a film. Its function is not only to generate awareness, but also to engage the viewer and create interest, ultimately influencing the consumer's purchase at the box office. From a marketing perspective, the creative process that goes into conceptualizing and designing a great movie poster is a crucial element contributing to what makes up a successful campaign. Obviously, this is all well and good, but

what I really love about posters in general is their versatility in artfully communicating an idea to the viewer. A great poster can be anything from an illustrated masterpiece—conveying the film's characters and capturing the overall tone of a film—to a minimalistic teaser leaving the viewer with just enough information to arouse curiosity and intrigue. It's amazing how posters can communicate in such a broad way, but personally I'm typically drawn to the aesthetic qualities of a poster—the combination of illustration, design, and composition is what ultimately defines my work, as well as many of the posters that end up in my collection.

EMPIRE POPPIN

REBELS DROPPIN

UNA NUEVA DIMENSIÓN EN CHOQUE!

EL MISTERIO...
LA ANGUSTIA...
EL HORROR...
PALPITAN EN
CADA ESCENA!

VEA:
LA DANZA
SENSUAL-
DE LA
MUERTE!

NADA LE
ATERRORIZARÁ
MAS QUE...

Un Película de
JESS FRANCO
con
ESTELLA BLAIN
HOWARD VERNON
MABEL KARR

MISS MUERTE

AVISO: Esta película es para la gente con los nervios del acero!

HITMAN
AGENT 47
IN THEATERS AUGUST 21

NEXUS-6 N6FAB61216
ZHORA

REPLICANT ⬡

MENTAL LEVEL B
PHYSICAL A

DIRECTIVE:
RETIRE

レプリカントを引退

全国高校

あなたは本気ですか

A FILM BY RIDLEY SCOTT

BLADE RUNNER

人間よりも人間

MATT DAMON

THE MARTIAN
DIRECTED BY RIDLEY SCOTT

EDGAR ASCENSÃO
www.posterspy.com/profile/edgarascensao

When I was a little kid and my mother sent me to bed as I was hypnotized on TV watching endless movies, she barely dreamed that I would be even more exhilarated by this love for cinema. At school I was like the cinema guru, the guy who would go to the bus with VHS tapes in his coat pockets to lend movies to friends. At home I was making homemade VHS covers, drawings, and collages to complete and proudly enhance my video library. Twenty years later, the knowledge is different but my passion has not slowed down. I combined my pleasure for drawing and illustration with my movie addiction. Alternative movie posters were the foundation of my new future. I grew up collecting reprints of some of the most famous movie posters of movie history. Classic poster examples like *Indiana Jones*,

Back to the Future, or *Blade Runner* gave me the urge to make art of my own. New artists and designers of the last decade are always inspiring me to do better, creating an art so profound that it embraces a cultural phenomenon across the world.

In 2009, I developed a Facebook page about my art (@posterscaseiros) and since then I've published two books thanks to crowdfunding. Regarding the projects I'm involved in, I always prefer working on movies I love, usually those I grew up with, from the '80s and '90s, some of them unknown or forgotten. Because, first and foremost, I create the poster for myself instead of others. It's like an artistic purge taking away what I've kept inside me.

TOM HANKS
FORR
EST
GUMP
DIRECTED BY ROBERT ZEMECKIS

BAD
MOTHER
FUCKER
A QUENTIN TARANTINO FILM
JOHN TRAVOLTA
SAMUEL L. JACKSON
UMA THURMAN
HARVEY KEITEL
TIM ROTH
AMANDA PLUMMER
MARIA DE MEDEIROS
VING RHAMES
ERIC STOLTZ
ROSANNA ARQUETTE
CHRISTOPHER WALKEN
BRUCE WILLIS
PULP FICTION
MIRAMAX FILMS PRESENTS A BAND APART AND JERSEY FILMS PRODUCTION A FILM BY QUENTIN TARANTINO "PULP FICTION" MUSIC SUPERVISION BY KARYN RACHTMAN
COSTUME DESIGNER BETSY HEIMANN PRODUCTION DESIGNER DAVID WASCO EDITED BY SALLY MENKE DIRECTOR OF PHOTOGRAPHY ANDRZEJ SEKULA
CO-EXECUTIVE PRODUCER BOB WEINSTEIN HARVEY WEINSTEIN RICHARD N. GLADSTEIN EXECUTIVE PRODUCER DANNY DEVITO MICHAEL SHAMBERG STACY SHER
MIRAMAX
STORY BY QUENTIN TARANTINO & ROGER AVARY PRODUCED BY LAWRENCE BENDER WRITTEN AND DIRECTED BY QUENTIN TARANTINO
18

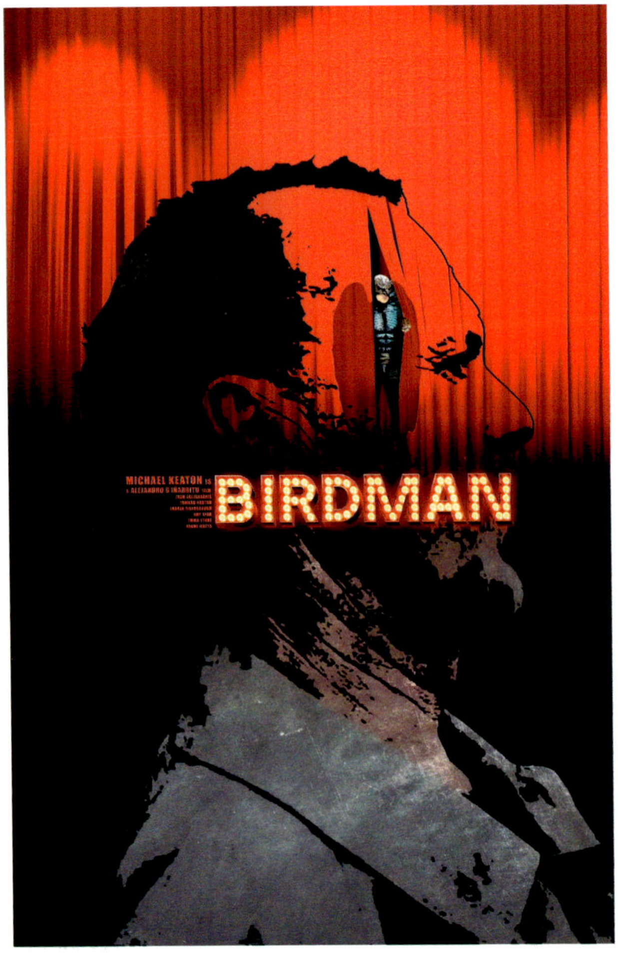
MICHAEL KEATON IS
A ALEJANDRO G IÑARRITU FILM
BIRDMAN

A STEVEN SPIELBERG FILM
BRIDGE OF SPIES
TOM HANKS
MARK RYLANCE
AMY RYAN
ALAN ALDA

CRISTOPHER A NOLAN FILM

INTERSTELLAR

FELIX TINDALL
www.felixtindall.com
www.posterspy.com/profile/shrimpy99

Movies have always inspired me. Whether it's the storytelling, the cinematography, the music, or the characters, it has the power to be so influential. I can't direct, I can't animate, I can't compose, and I can barely write or edit. But

I feel the least I can do to pay tribute to the awesome culture and it's fans, is to channel that inspiration into creating poster designs inspired by some of my favorites!

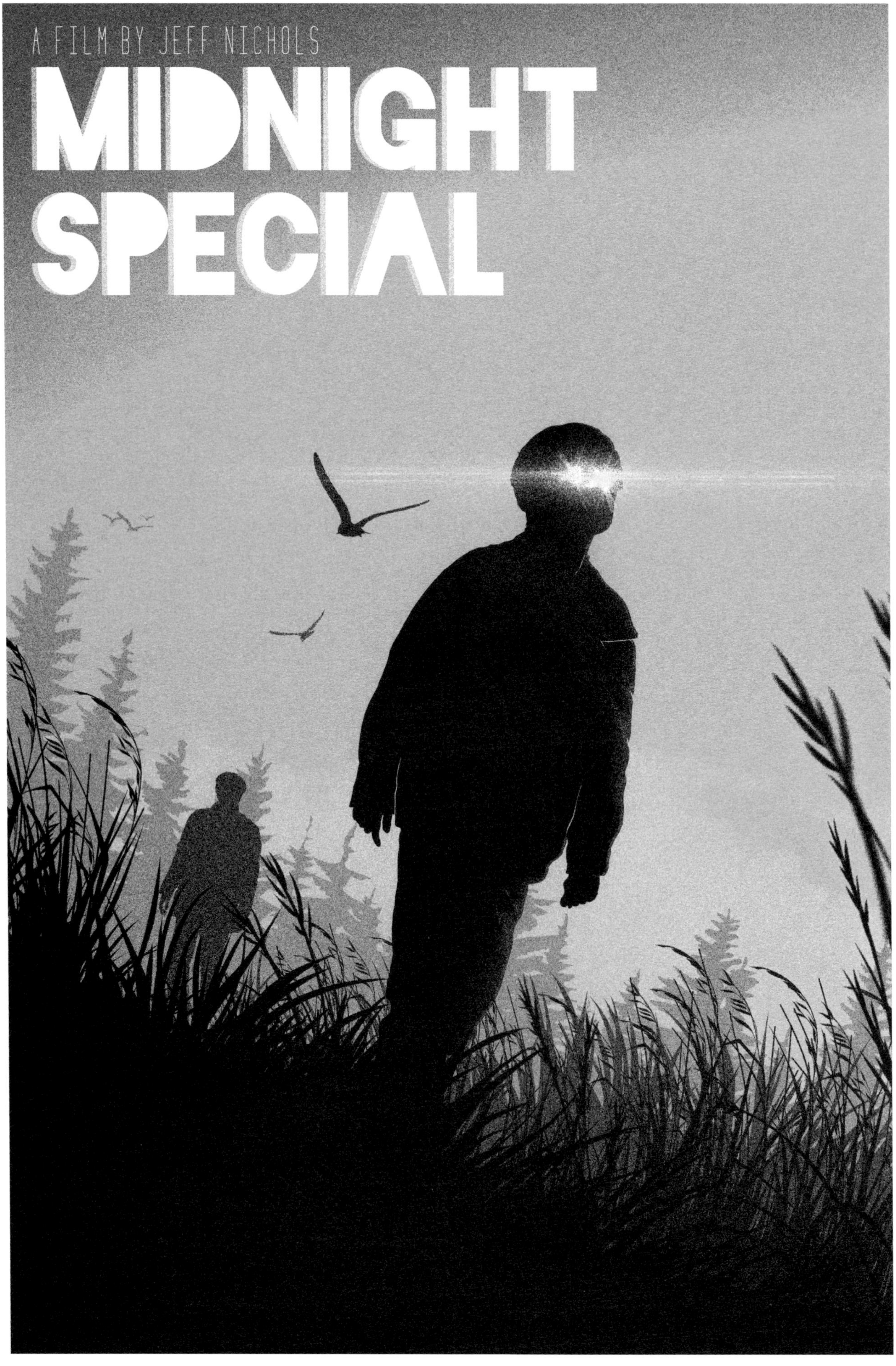
A FILM BY JEFF NICHOLS
MIDNIGHT SPECIAL

MATT DAMON

THE MARTIAN

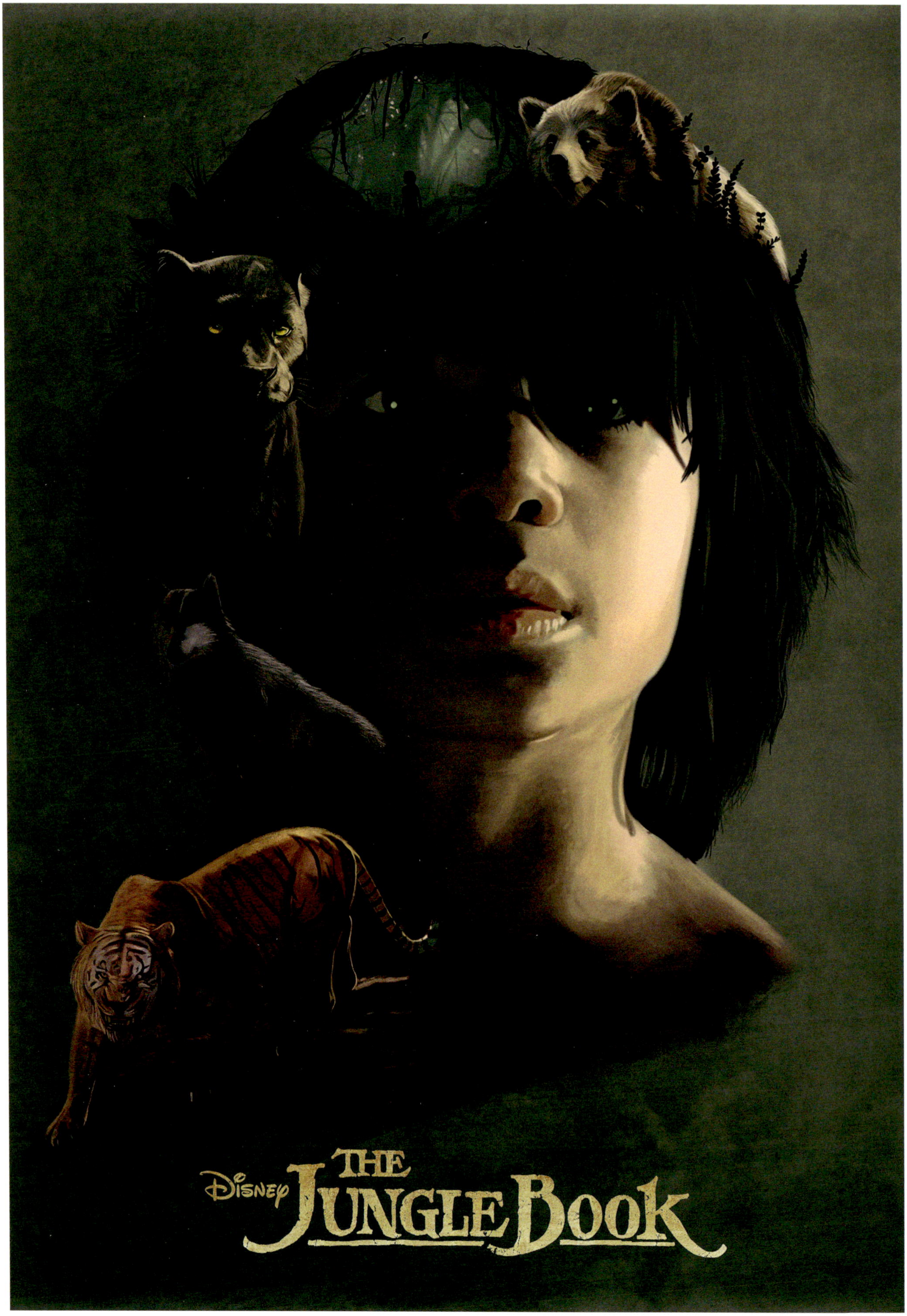
Disney
THE
JUNGLE BOOK

FREYA BETTS
freyabetts.co.uk
www.posterspy.com/profile/freyabetts

In my spare time I love to create digital art and recently I have been focusing on alternative film posters. I always try and keep my technique as close to fine art as possible by drawing freehand, I love the illustrative approach when it comes to film poster design. Working in the film industry, I can see that illustration is something that is no longer commonplace in commercial poster design, and is a medium I enjoy bringing back into the art of film posters.

Crimson Peak

GIUSEPPE
BALESTRA

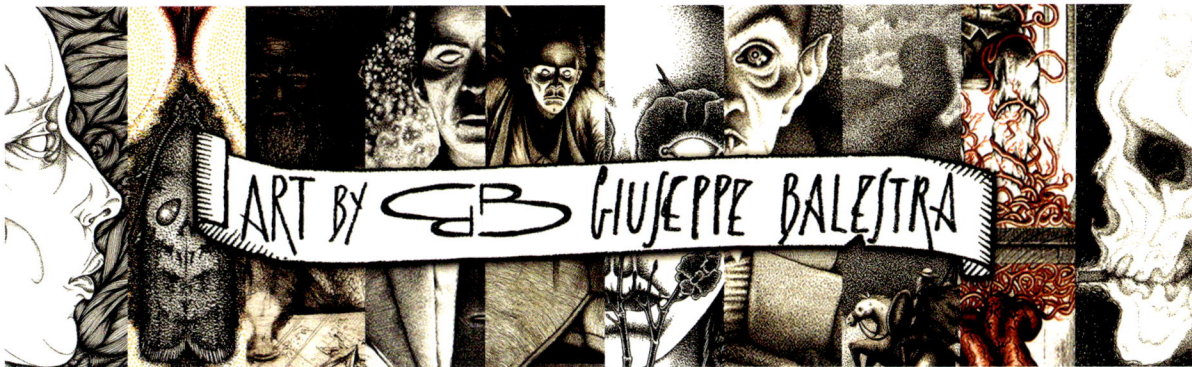

GIUSEPPE BALESTRA
www.facebook.com/ARTbyGB
www.posterspy.com/profile/GiuseppeBalestraArt

I'm an Italian illustrator. I generally work in pen and ink, hatching and stippling, creating illustrations usually inspired by literature or movies. I'm fascinated by the way a movie poster can hold the whole meaning of a film. With a single image the observer can be fully taken in by the movie's atmosphere.

If you have seen the movie, a poster can play with your knowledge of the plot, evoking emotions and feelings in you; it can establish a sort of complicity with you because you are able to understand the double meanings of the image. On the other hand, if you haven't seen the movie, a poster has the power to intrigue you and make you feel the need to watch it, the need to know more about it, the need to be part of that mysterious world.

That's why I like to create movie posters that tell a little story, usually presenting a character or a particular element that I think is capable of evoking interest, but without revealing too much about the plot and of course avoiding unnecessary spoilers. Not everything has to be clear, you have to discover it yourself.

I usually draw my posters in ink, eventually adding digital color because I want to give them a tangible look. I think that if a poster has a handmade look, it's more simple to sympathize with it.

if it's in a word
or in a look
you can't get rid of

THE
Ba bA Dook

BRAD PITT
Melanie Laurent
MICHAEL FASSBENDER
CHRISTOPH WALTZ
ELI ROTH
A FILM BY
QUENTIN TARANTINO
INGLOURIOUS BASTERDS

HOWARD
THE DUCK

GEORGE LUCAS PRESENTS A WILLARD HUYCK FILM A GLORIA KATZ PRODUCTION
STARRING LEA THOMPSON   JEFFREY JONES   TIM ROBBINS "HOWARD THE DUCK" WRITTEN BY WILLARD HUYCK AND GLORIA KATZ BASED ON A COMIC BY STEVE GERBER
MUSIC BY THOMAS DOLBY   CO-PRODUCER ROBERT LATHAM BROWN   EXECUTIVE PRODUCER GEORGE LUCAS   PRODUCER GLORIA KATZ   DIRECTED BY WILLARD HUYCK

LUCASFILM

UNIVERSAL

HARLAN ELAM
www.harlanelam.com
www.posterspy.com/profile/harlanelam

As a kid I loved waiting in the lobby of my local theater just to look in awe at the posters hanging before me. The vivid imagery would invite me to linger and imagine worlds and stories that waited in upcoming releases. I always aim to tell stories through my posters with the hope of inviting people into that same frame of mind full of childish wonder and imagination.

GODZILLA

ALIEN

20TH CENTURY FOX PRESENTS
SIGOURNEY WEAVER · TOM SKERRITT · VERONICA CARTWRIGHT
HARRY DEAN STANTON · JOHN HURT · IAN HOLM AND YAPHET KOTTO AS PARKER
ALIEN · PRODUCED BY GORDON CARROLL · DAVID GILER AND WALTER HILL
SCREENPLAY BY DAN O'BANNON · STORY BY RONALD SHUSETT · CINEMATOGRAPHY DEREK VANLINT
MUSIC BY JERRY GOLDSMITH · EDITING BY TERRY RAWLINGS AND PETER WEATHERLEY
DIRECTED BY RIDLEY SCOTT

WALL·E

M E N

DAYS OF FUTURE PAST

KILLED   CAUGHT

FURY ROAD

CHRISTOPHER NOLAN

INTERSTELLAR

Disney
BIG
HERO
6

GET IN.
GET OUT.
STAY ALIVE.

BRYAN CRANSTON IS
THE INFILTRATOR

BENJAMIN BRATT AS "ROBERTO ALCAINO"
JOHN LEGUIZAMO AS "EMIR ABREU"
DIANE KRUGER AS "KATHY ERTZ"

BROADGREEN
PICTURES

Directed and Produced by BRAD FURMAN   Screenplay by ELLEN BROWN FURMAN
Based on the book by ROBERT MAZUR

My dad loves cinema, so he was always choosing nice films in the video store next to my house for my brother and me to watch.
I grew up in the '80s, so that means a lot of timeless classics! It was also the moment when video games were becoming more and more popular—both console and computer games, particularly graphic adventures. Computer-generated images were not broadly used at the time so all the video games and VHS tapes would have beautifully illustrated covers! It was also the time when my older brother began to read comic books. We would spend lots of Saturday afternoons laying on the rug in silence drawing our favorite Marvel or Dragon Ball characters. After those years I stopped painting for a while.

I tried doing other stuff but those memories would always come back as some of the most peaceful moments of my childhood. In a way, drawing movie posters transports me to a moment in time where every day would bring something new to discover, full of possibilities.

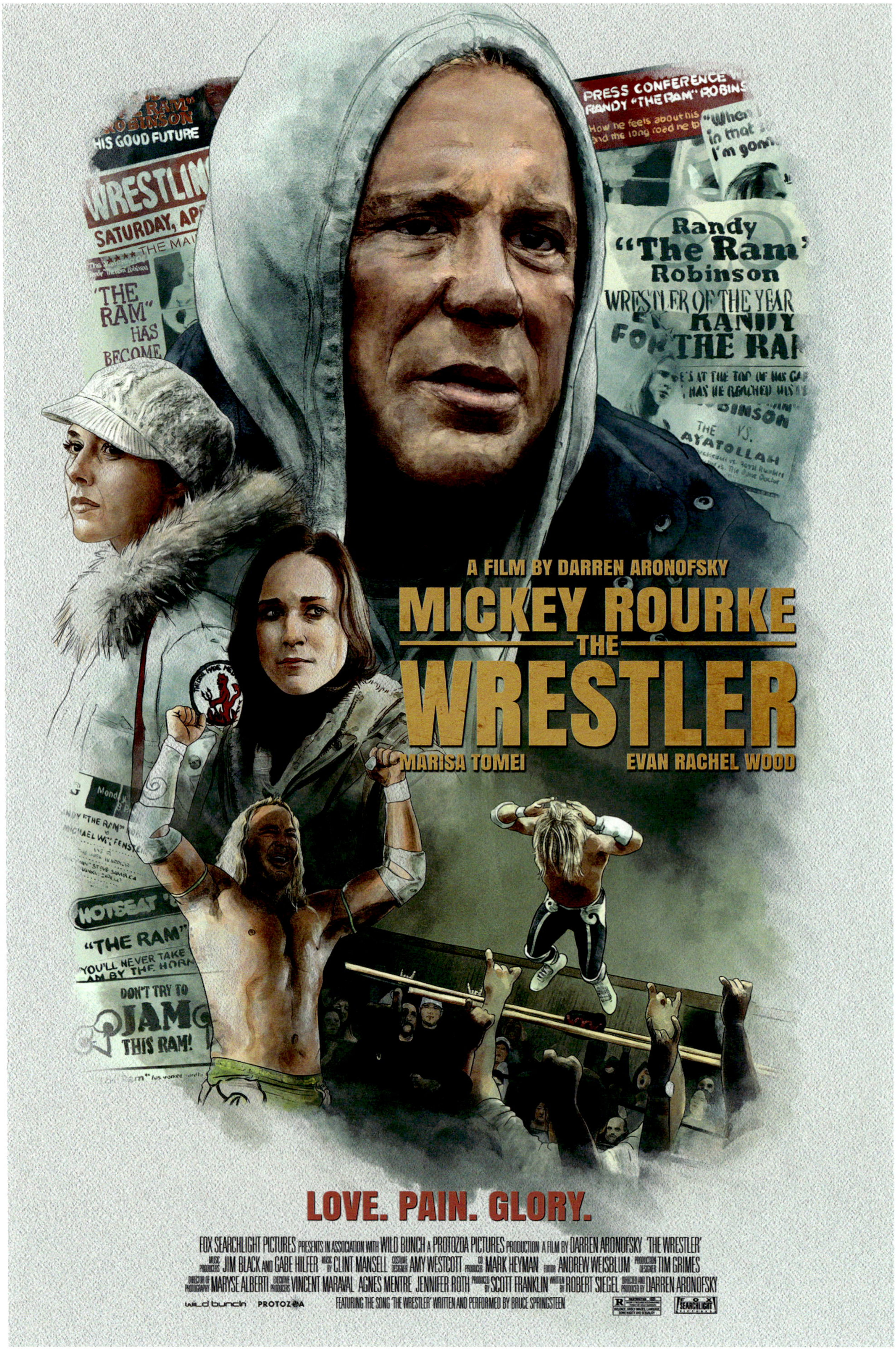
A FILM BY DARREN ARONOFSKY
MICKEY ROURKE
THE
WRESTLER
MARISA TOMEI
EVAN RACHEL WOOD
LOVE. PAIN. GLORY.
FOX SEARCHLIGHT PICTURES PRESENTS IN ASSOCIATION WITH WILD BUNCH A PROTOZOA PICTURES PRODUCTION A FILM BY DARREN ARONOFSKY 'THE WRESTLER'
MUSIC PRODUCERS JIM BLACK AND GABE HILFER MUSIC BY CLINT MANSELL COSTUME DESIGNER AMY WESTCOTT CO PRODUCER MARK HEYMAN EDITOR ANDREW WEISBLUM PRODUCTION DESIGNER TIM GRIMES
DIRECTOR OF PHOTOGRAPHY MARYSE ALBERTI EXECUTIVE PRODUCERS VINCENT MARAVAL AGNES MENTRE JENNIFER ROTH PRODUCED BY SCOTT FRANKLIN WRITTEN BY ROBERT SIEGEL DIRECTED AND PRODUCED BY DARREN ARONOFSKY
FEATURING THE SONG 'THE WRESTLER' WRITTEN AND PERFORMED BY BRUCE SPRINGSTEEN

Inside Llewyn Davis
OSCAR ISAAC
CAREY MULLIGAN
JOHN GOODMAN
GARRETT HEDLUND
JUSTIN TIMBERLAKE
WRITTEN AND DIRECTED BY JOEL & ETHAN COEN
CBS FILMS AND STUDIOCANAL PRESENT IN ASSOCIATION WITH ANTON CAPITAL ENTERTAINMENT OSCAR ISAAC CAREY MULLIGAN JOHN GOODMAN GARRETT HEDLUND
F. MURRAY ABRAHAM AND JUSTIN TIMBERLAKE "INSIDE LLEWYN DAVIS" ELLEN CHENOWETH T BONE BURNETT RODERICK JAYNES MARY ZOPHRES
JESS GONCHOR BRUNO DELBONNEL, A.F.C., A.S.C. ROBERT GRAF OLIVIER COURSON RON HALPERN SCOTT RUDIN ETHAN COEN JOEL COEN
STUDIOCANAL
ACE
ETHAN COEN JOEL COEN
CBS FILMS
www.ignaciorc.com

THE
WOLF
OF
WALL
STREET

JAVIER VERA LAINEZ
www.javierveralainez.com
www.posterspy.com/profile/javierveralainez

My grandad always wondered how I could earn enough money to live drawing with my computer. I never knew how to answer his question, but at the same time I couldn't imagine another way. After some years of drawing and designing for others (God bless my clients), I needed my own project, just for fun. I tried many different things. One day I did an alternative poster for *Big Fish* and uploaded it to my Facebook page. My friends liked it and started to suggest new titles, "You should do that movie . . . you must do a film by this director . . . you HAVE to . . . ." I did not listen too much to them, but it became a great way to conceptualize arguments, to find a visual key for a whole story, and I really liked that. I evolved a lot in my work. In the end, it also made me a very busy person. And happier.

PSYCHO

THE TEXAS CHAINSAW MASSACRE

THE SHINING

LADYHAWKE

91

BONE TOMAHAWK

JEREMY WHEELER
www.thisisbangmedia.com
www.posterspy.com/profile/jeremywheeler

I grew up a mini movie buff who was always dazzled by movie posters. They could be dynamic, subdued, sum up a film with a montage, or present a mystery that made you curious about the film. They were my first inklings of what a movie was; sometimes seen in the theater lobby, other times in publications like *Starlog*, *Fangoria*, or *Premiere Magazine*—nevermind all of the glimpses stolen from video store racks (when the poster was used for the box art, that is). As the alt film poster movement came on the scene, I was given the opportunity to adapt the films that I love with my own signature art—some through art galleries (most notably, Hero Complex Gallery in Los Angeles), and some official, as with my

prints for FrightFest Originals and LP art for DeathWaltz Recording Company I swayed more towards comic book-style illustration, with other inspirations ranging from dynamic international movie poster layouts to lifelong idols such as the great American poster illustrators Bob Peak and Bill Sienkiewicz, the comic art legend whose work redefined comics as an art form. As for modern designers, I tend to respect most those who are evoking the feel of the '70s — people like Jay Shaw, Brandon Schaefer, and Midnight Marauder. I'm especially happy that Francesco Francavilla has found acclaim for his movie art, as he represents a direct link from comics to films, and I tend to love just about everything he does.

EVIL DEAD II

RENAISSANCE PICTURES PRESENTS 'EVIL DEAD II' STARRING BRUCE CAMPBELL WITH SARAH BERRY • DAN HICKS • KASSIE WESLEY • RICHARD DOMEIER •
MUSIC BY JOSEPH LO DUCA • SPECIAL EFFECTS MAKEUP BY MARK SHOSTROM • EDITED BY KAYE DAVIS • DIRECTOR OF PHOTOGRAPHY PETER DEMING •
EXECUTIVE PRODUCERS IRVIN SHAPIRO • ALEX De BENEDETTI • WRITTEN BY SAM RAIMI • SCOTT SPIEGEL • PRODUCED BY ROBERT TAPERT •
DIRECTED BY SAM RAIMI

NO IDEAS

DOUBT HUMANITY

BUY

SLEEP

FOLLOW

LIKE CONSUME

SUBMIT

CONFORM

EAT

NO INDEPENDENT THOUGHT

CONNECT

SURRENDER

WATCH TV

STREAM

MARRY AND REPRODUCE

OBEY

SLE

NO

THIS IS YOUR GOD

JOHN CARPENTER'S

THEY LIVE

ALIVE FILMS PRESENTS A LARRY FRANCO PRODUCTION
JOHN CARPENTER'S 'THEY LIVE' RODDY PIPER • KEITH DAVID • MEG FOSTER
SCREENPLAY BY FRANK ARMITAGE MUSIC BY JOHN CARPENTER AND ALAN HOWARTH
DIRECTOR OF PHOTOGRAPHY GARY B. KIBBE EXECUTIVE PRODUCERS SHEP GORDON AND ANDRE BLAY
ASSOCIATE PRODUCER SANDY KING PRODUCED BY LARRY FRANCO DIRECTED BY JOHN CARPENTER

OUTSIDE THE LIMIT
OF OUR SIGHT, THEY LIVE.

FFO
FRIGHTFEST ORIGINALS

IN SPACE NO ONE CAN HEAR YOU SCREAM.

A RIDLEY SCOTT FILM

ALIEN

R | RESTRICTED
UNDER 17 REQUIRES ACCOMPANYING
PARENT OR ADULT GUARDIAN

JOHN ASLARONA
www.johnaslarona.com
www.posterspy.com/profile/johnaslarona

Back in my youth, I remember having a bunch of mounted posters at home. I thought then it was just cool to have them hanging around to add some color to the wall. Over the years I've come to appreciate them more for what they are. As some would see posters only as a marketing tool, I think that great poster art, design, or slogan for films can be as iconic as the movies—they become part of it in so many ways. It fascinates me how posters invite and introduce us to the films, the characters, how they grab our attention, compel us to think, feel emotions, or be curious about something we have yet to experience, or remind us of something familiar. As artists, when we are entertained or compelled, we are inspired to create or recreate visuals of our own and in some manner, we pay forward that kind of fascination or feelings and hope to inspire creativity and tickle that nostalgia bone.

THE DARK KNIGHT

SUICIDE SQUAD

STEPHEN KING'S
IT

MAD
MAX
FURY ROAD
VILLAGE ROADSHOW PICTURES
KENNEDY MILLER MITCHELL
WATERTOWER MUSIC
MAY 15
Facebook.com/madmaxmovie
Madmaxmovie.com #MadMax
WARNER BROS. PICTURES

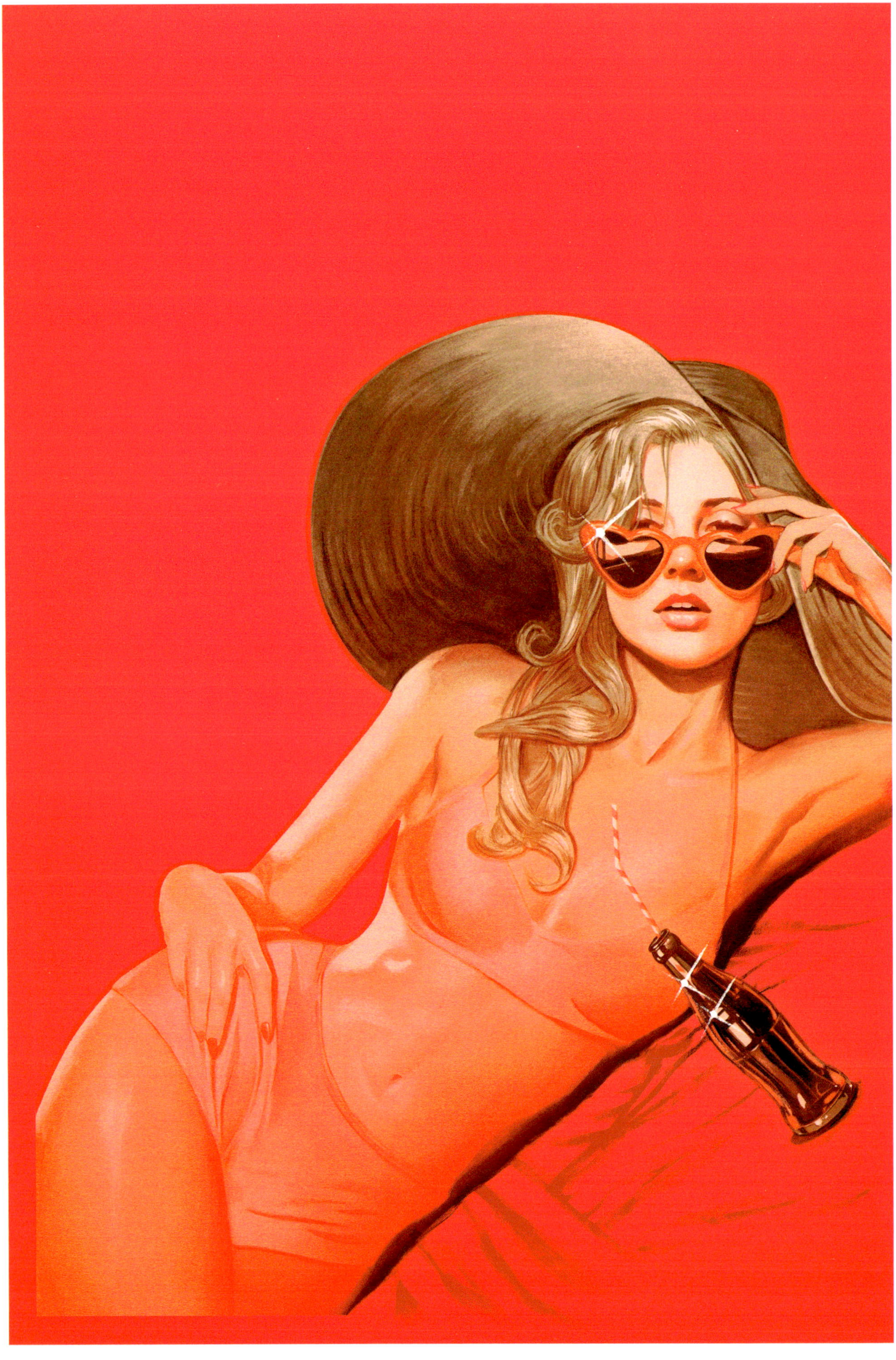

JOHN KEAVENEY
www.johnkeaveneydesigns.com
www.posterspy.com/profile/223_john

Movie posters are one of my favorite forms of art as well as comics. Movie posters tell the notion of the story, characters, and theme in one image. My childhood faves instilled magic and are masterpieces of their time. Classics by legendary artists like Drew Struzan, John Alvin, and Bob Peak have inspired me since I was a child. These posters have become unforgettable pieces that throw me back to the much-loved films of my childhood. I couldn't pick a favorite, there are so many! Over the years I've created works for many clients and have been fortunate to work at a film company producing official posters. Now I create my own work and look to produce licensed prints that emulate a retro illustration style. With my work I generally focus on the protagonist focal point for communicating the idea and narrative.

STAR WARS
THE FORCE AWAKENS

DRACULA

ART BY JOHN KEAVENEY

102

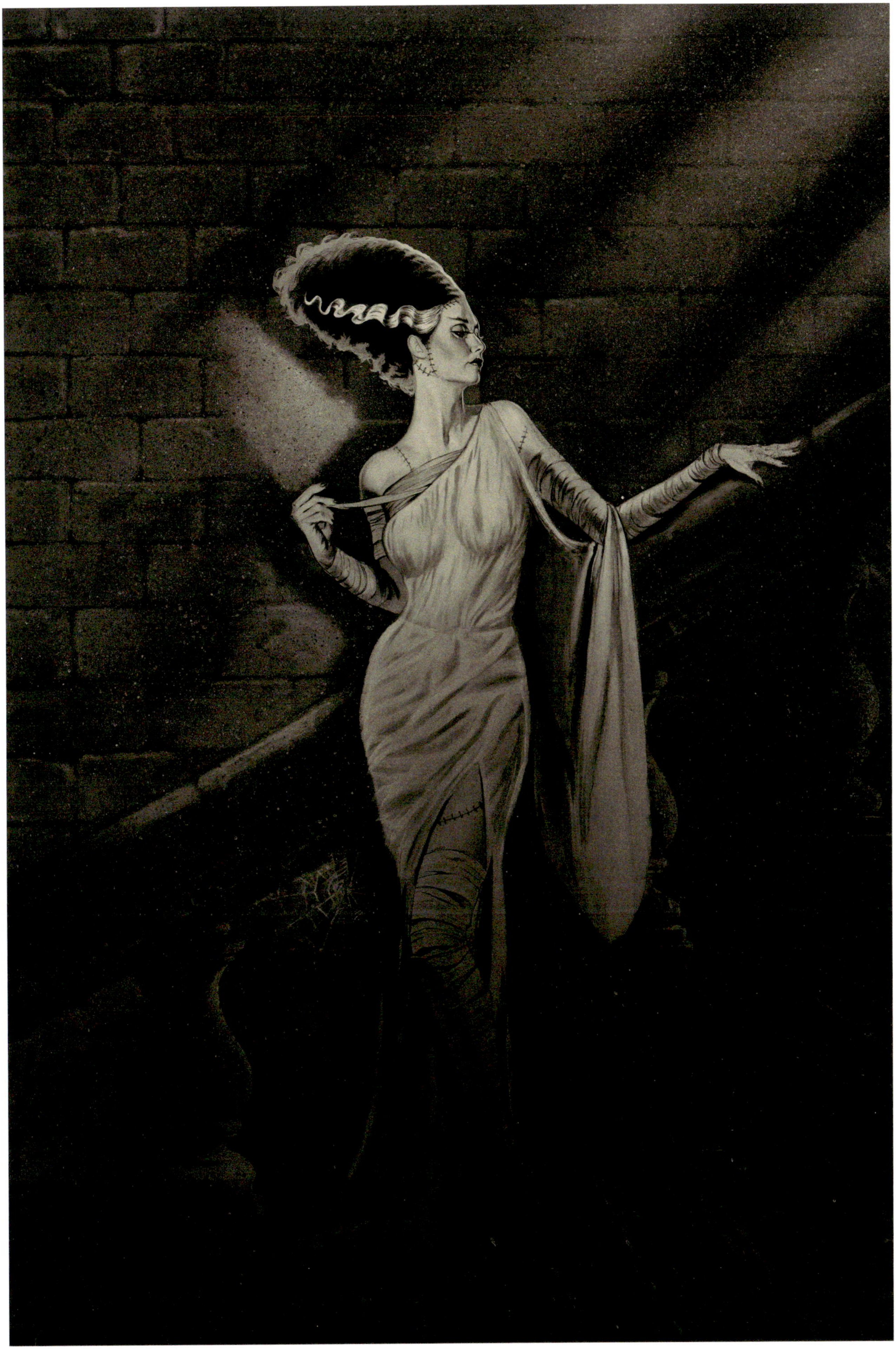

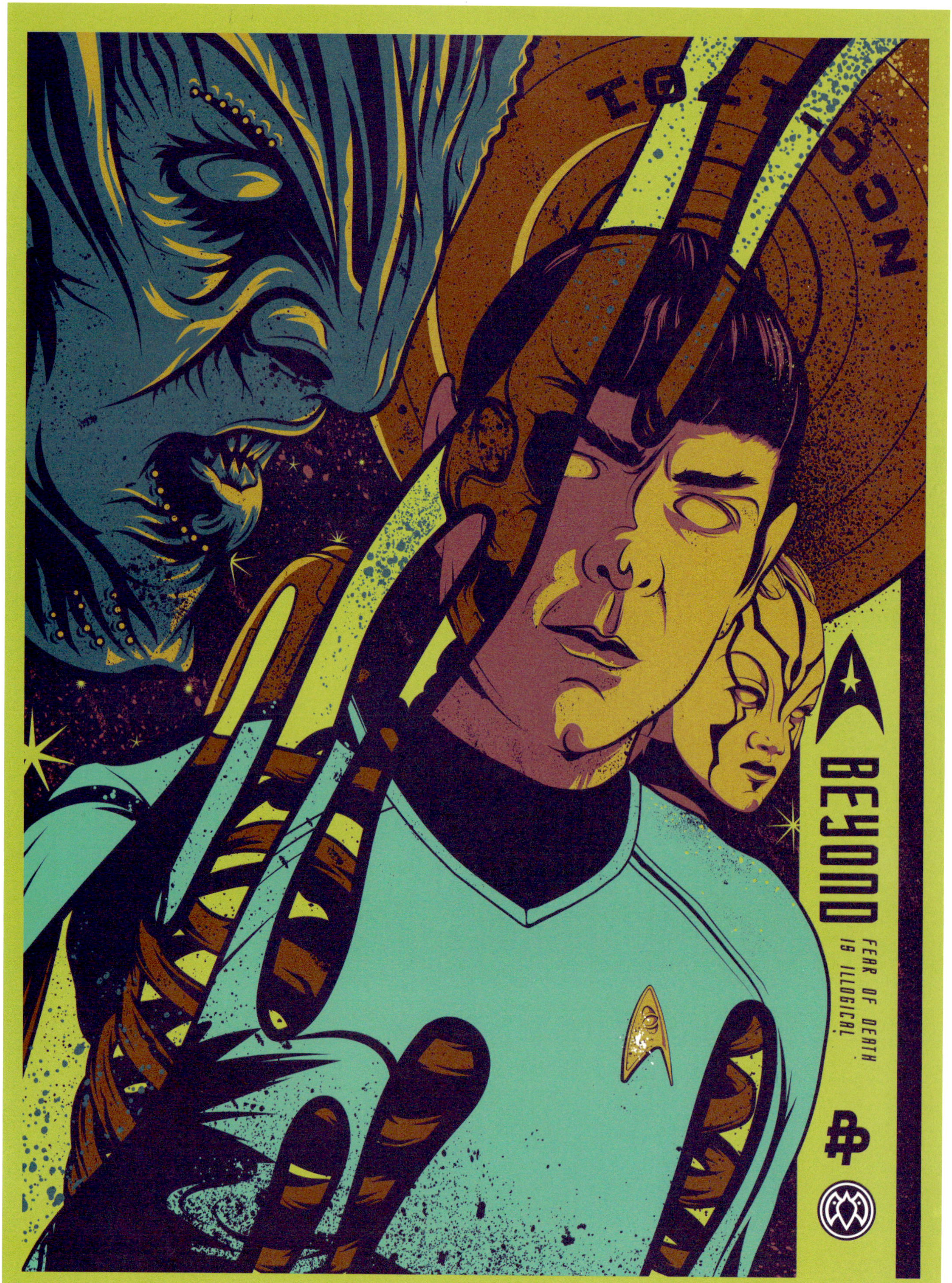
BEYOND
FEAR OF DEATH
IS ILLOGICAL.

JOSH CAMPBELL
www.paybackpenguin.com
www.posterspy.com/profile/paybackpenguin

I am an illustrator and designer based in Nebraska, USA. A majority of my poster projects are inspired by pure passion for the movies. To create a broader perspective I seek out other designers to partner with because this type of collaboration helps me grow as an artist and inspires me to have fun with a subject. As an artist, illustrating a movie poster helps me convey my interpretation of the story. It's never a complete story and thus is left to the viewer to further interpret. With my own interpretation I strive to deepen the emotion of what plays out in theaters. For me, several of my pieces are based on the idea of loneliness. This lonely hero who gives the viewer a central figure of focus and thus creates an emotional, often deeper, unspoken story not obviously played out.

THE JUDGE

PAYBACK PENGUIN

TEENAGE MUTANT NINJA TURTLES

LEADER

VIG

PAYBACK PENGUIN

TMNT 25TH ANNIVERSARY

TWENTIETH CENTURY FOX PRESENTS "SPEED"

KEANU REEVES DENNIS HOPPER SANDRA BULLOCK

PRODUCED BY MARK GORDON EXECUTIVE PRODUCER IAN BRYCE WRITTEN BY GRAHAM YOST

MUSIC BY MARK MANCINA POSTER BY JOSH CAMPBELL

R RESTRICTED
UNDER 17 REQUIRES ACCOMPANYING
PARENT OR ADULT GUARDIAN

RESTRICTED
UNDER 17 REQUIRES ACCOMPANYING
PARENT OR ADULT GUARDIAN

PARAMOUNT PICTURES PRESENTS A LAWRENCE GORDON PRODUCTION "THE WARRIORS"
EXECUTIVE PRODUCER FRANK MARSHALL   BASED UPON THE NOVEL BY SOL YURICK
SCREENPLAY BY DAVID SHABER AND WALTER HILL   PRODUCED BY LAWRENCE GORDON
DIRECTED BY WALTER HILL

Paramount
A Paramount Communications Company

THE WARRIORS

JOSHUA KELLY (J-MONSTER ART)

jmonsterart.co.uk
www.posterspy.com/profile/j-monster-art

Movie posters are a great way of giving the audience insight on a film through the medium of illustration. I love posters—movie trailers can often give too much away. I am a massive movie fan and cinema-goer, but the official posters just don't catch my eye like the alternative ones do. When I found out there was a whole community for this type of artwork, I wanted to be a part of it. To put your own spin on some of your favorite and cult classic films is so enjoyable.

SWISS ARMY MAN

PAUL DANO   DANIEL RADCLIFFE

An A24 release TADMOR and ASTRAKAN FILMS AB present a COLD IRON PICTURES BLACKBIRD FILMS production in association with DELUXE ENTERTAINMENT SERVICES GROUP
A FILM BY DANIELS starring PAUL DANO DANIEL RADCLIFFE and MARY ELIZABETH WINSTEAD "SWISS ARMY MAN"
music by ANDY HULL and ROBERT MCDOWELL costume designer STEPHANI LEWIS production designer JASON KISVARDAY editor MATTHEW HANNAM, CCE director of photography LARKIN SEIPLE
co producer TODD KING executive producers GIDEON TADMOR JIM KAUFMAN WILLIAM OLSSON producers EYAL RIMMON LAUREN MANN produced by LAWRENCE INGLEE P.G.A. JONATHAN WANG P.G.A. MIRANDA BAILEY AMANDA MARSHALL
written and directed by DANIEL SCHEINERT and DANIEL KWAN

BRYAN CRANSTON

THE INFILTRATOR

IN CINEMAS SEPTEMBER 16

110

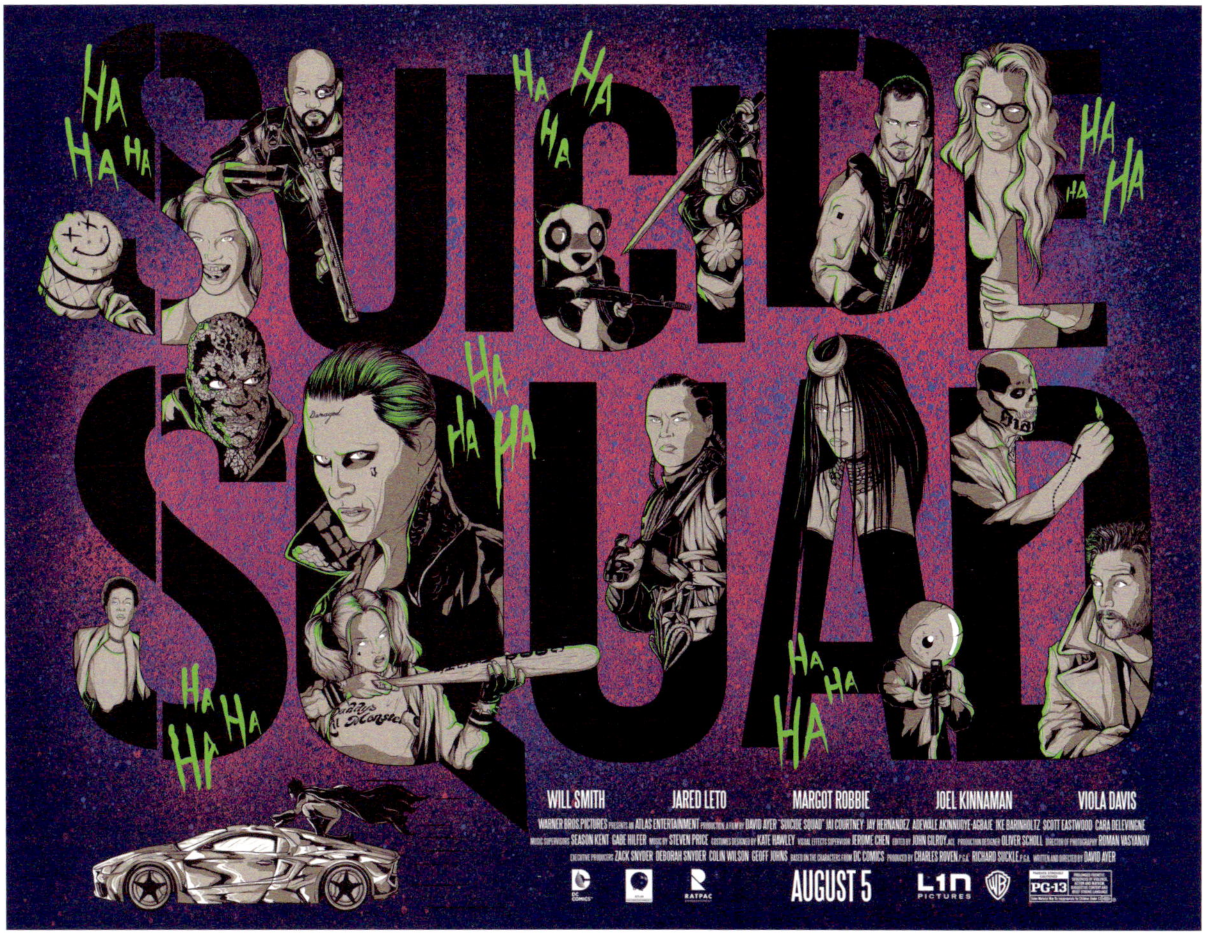
SUICIDE SQUAD
HA HA HA
WILL SMITH JARED LETO MARGOT ROBBIE JOEL KINNAMAN VIOLA DAVIS
WARNER BROS.PICTURES PRESENTS AN ATLAS ENTERTAINMENT PRODUCTION A FILM BY DAVID AYER "SUICIDE SQUAD" JAI COURTNEY JAY HERNANDEZ ADEWALE AKINNUOYE-AGBAJE IKE BARINHOLTZ SCOTT EASTWOOD CARA DELEVINGNE
MUSIC SUPERVISORS SEASON KENT GABE HILFER MUSIC BY STEVEN PRICE COSTUMES DESIGNED BY KATE HAWLEY VISUAL EFFECTS SUPERVISOR JEROME CHEN EDITED BY JOHN GILROY, A.C.E. PRODUCTION DESIGNER OLIVER SCHOLL DIRECTOR OF PHOTOGRAPHY ROMAN VASYANOV
EXECUTIVE PRODUCERS ZACK SNYDER DEBORAH SNYDER COLIN WILSON GEOFF JOHNS BASED ON THE CHARACTERS FROM DC COMICS PRODUCED BY CHARLES ROVEN, P.G.A. RICHARD SUCKLE, P.G.A. WRITTEN AND DIRECTED BY DAVID AYER
DC COMICS
RATPAC
AUGUST 5
L1N PICTURES
PG-13

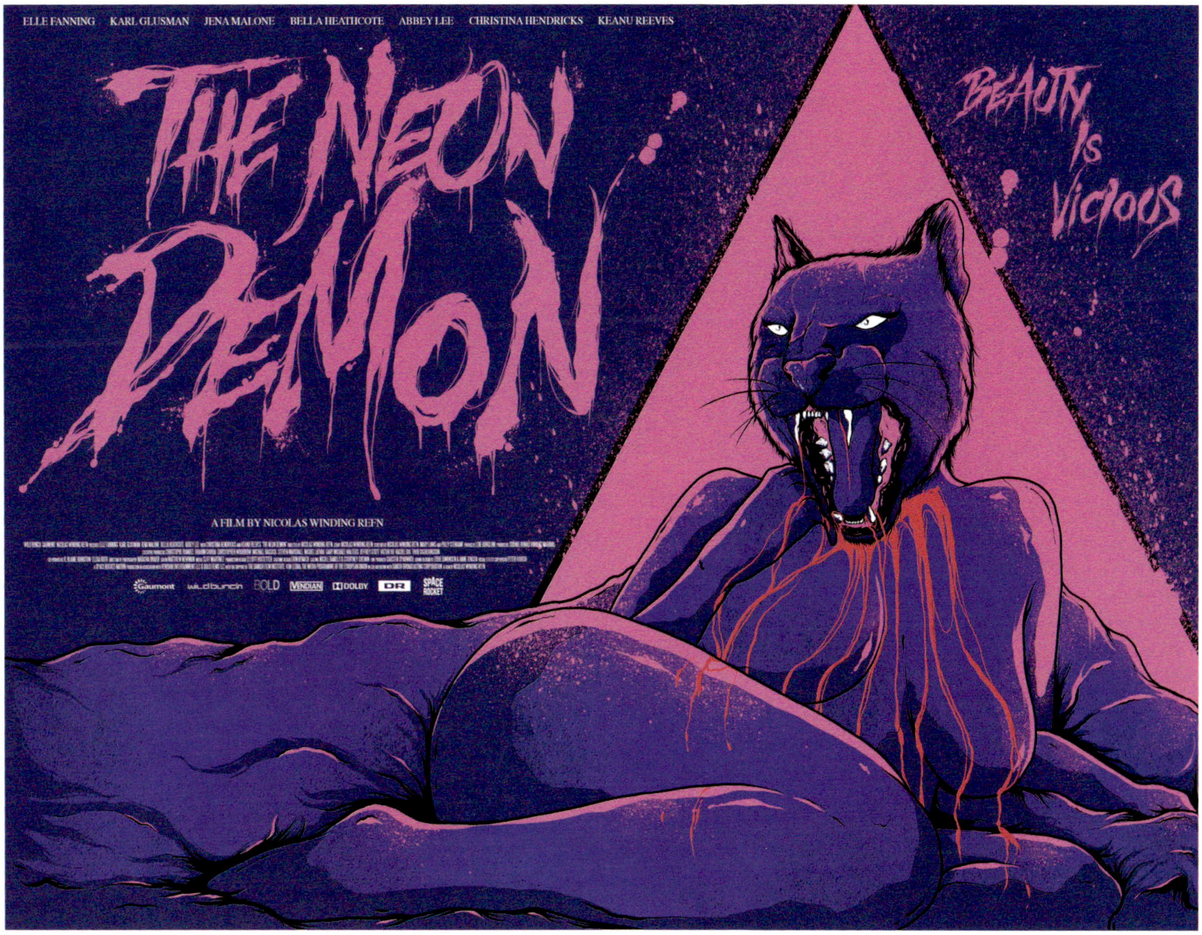
ELLE FANNING KARL GLUSMAN JENA MALONE BELLA HEATHCOTE ABBEY LEE CHRISTINA HENDRICKS KEANU REEVES
THE NEON DEMON
BEAUTY IS VICIOUS
A FILM BY NICOLAS WINDING REFN

THE LEGO BATMAN MOVIE

KEVIN TIERNAN
www. tiernandesign.com
www.posterspy.com/profile/kevintiernan

I became interested in alternative movie art because of *Jurassic Park* and *Guardians of the Galaxy*. Mondo had an incredible *Jurassic Park* release, then *Guardians* hit theaters later that year. I love how different artists lend their unique style to iconic scenes and characters. Even if something came out twenty years ago, you still have a chance to put your own spin on elements from the story. While a group of fans might all be watching the same film, everybody can have a fresh perspective on it. Movies can make us feel like we're a piece of something bigger. That's one of the best aspects of creating prints and fan art. There's a sense of community drawing people together by what they're passionate about. After a trailer premiers online, it's always cool to watch the flood of new artwork. Posters can be fun, effective ways to capture the spirit of a movie and connect with others.

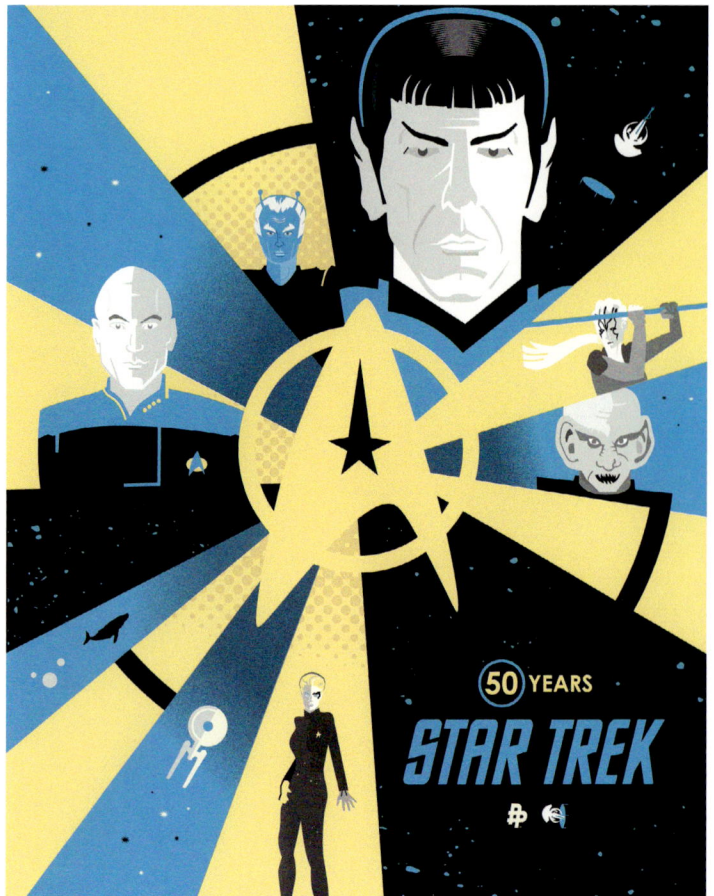

Tom Hanks is
Forrest Gump

LADISLAS

www.ladislasdesign.com
www.posterspy.com/profile/ladislas

Alternative movie posters are very important for me as they represented the path for me to begin a new career as an illustrator and digital artist. I used to be frustrated by what I was doing as a graphic designer. For many years I never took the time to learn how to draw and was limited in terms of creation. One day, I made the decision that I had to change. I love movies, some are very inspiring to me and I enjoy feeling immersed in their universes. I've discovered great artists like Drew Struzan who were making stunning art inspired by these movies. I told myself that it would be a great way to associate two of my passions: making art and movies.

That's how I started to draw more and create what I call graphic tributes to my favorite movies. I've committed myself to create artworks that are not traced. I use reference photos and then I draw each and every poster from scratch without using any photographs in it. Alternative posters are for me an experimentation lab where I can study portraits and enjoy the process as I create some tributes to movies I enjoyed watching. My goal in each of my posters is to create an artwork that will symbolize the atmosphere of the movie I've chosen to illustrate. This alternative movie poster scene is so exciting, it's hard to get bored with it.

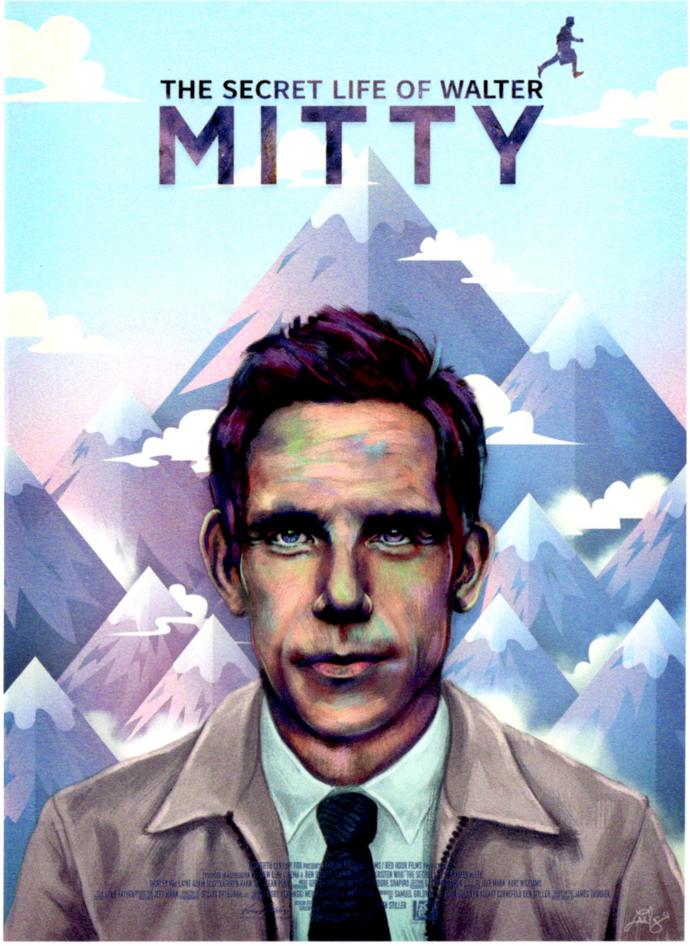
THE SECRET LIFE OF WALTER
MITTY

WILL SMITH TOMMY LEE JONES
MIB
MEN IN BLACK
COLUMBIA PICTURES
www.ladislasdesign.com

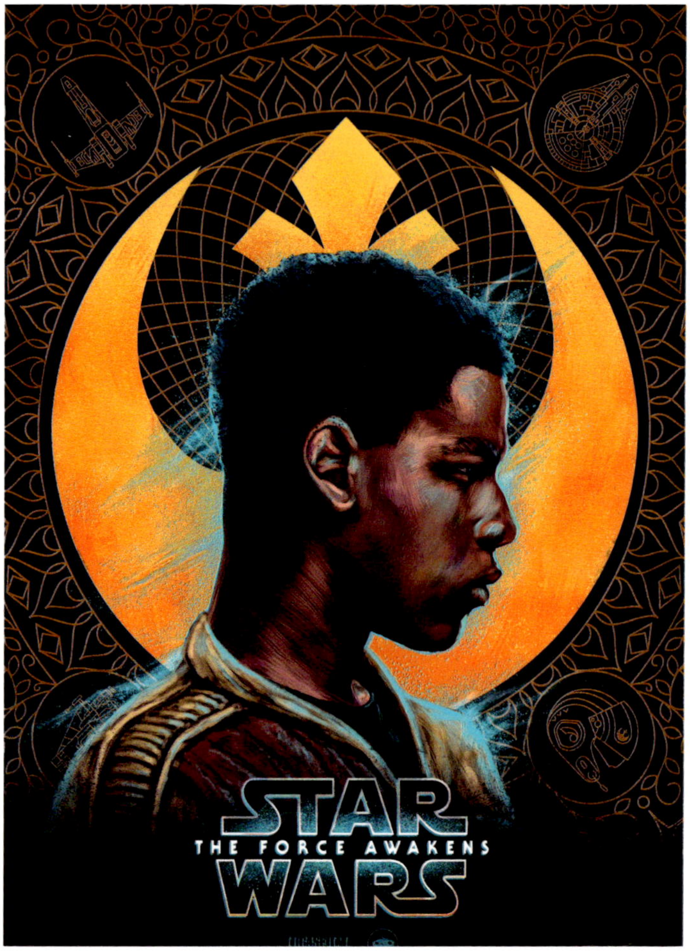
STAR
THE FORCE AWAKENS
WARS

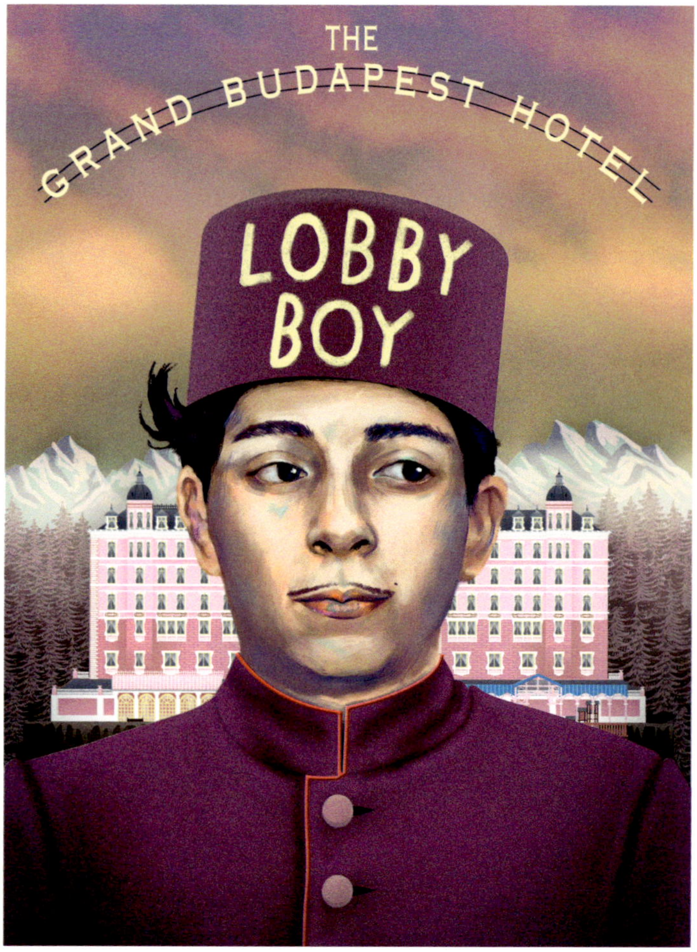
THE
GRAND BUDAPEST HOTEL
LOBBY
BOY

L'ODYSSÉE

UN FILM DE JÉRÔME SALLE

SPECTRE

ALBERT R. BROCCOLI'S EON PRODUCTIONS PRESENTS DANIEL CRAIG AS IAN FLEMING'S JAMES BOND 007 IN "SPECTRE" CHRISTOPH WALTZ LÉA SYDOUX BEN WHISHAW NAOMI HARRIS DAVID BAUTISTA WITH MONICA BELLUCI AND RALPH FIENNES AS "M" CO PRODUCERS DANIEL CRAIG ANDREW NOAKES DAVID POPE MUSIC BY THOMAS NEWMAN COSTUME DESIGNER JANY TEMIME EDITOR LEE SMITH ACE PRODUCTION DESIGNER DENNIS GASSNER DIRECTOR OF PHOTOGRAPHY HOYTE VAN HOYTEMA, FSF NSC EXECUTIVE PRODUCER CALLUM McDOUGALL STORY BY JOHN LOGAN and NEAL PURVIS & ROBERT WADE SCREENPLAY BY JOHN LOGAN and NEAL PURVIS & ROBERT WADE and JEZ BUTTERWORTH

MGM PRODUCED BY MICHAEL G. WILSON and BARBARA BROCCOLI DIRECTED BY SAM MENDES COLUMBIA PICTURES

FEATURING "WRITING'S ON THE WALL" PERFORMED BY SAM SMITH

NOVEMBER 6 2015

LAURA RACERO
www.lauraracero.com
www.posterspy.com/profile/lauraracero

The first time I used a pencil, I was three years old. And since then, I have not stopped drawing, either on paper or on a tablet. The film world caught my eye when I was a child. By then, the facades of movie theatres showed enormous and colorful reproductions of movie posters. And I always looked at them completely fascinated. The poster that made me fall in love with the profession was the one Richard Amsel designed for *Raiders of the Lost Ark*. And along with Amsel, Drew Struzan very quickly became an inspiration. In my first fan art pieces, I tried to imitate his style using digital techniques. Gradually, I moved away from that, finding my own style. It was a good decision and the result of a natural evolution. However, film posters were just a hobby, a way out to deal with my daily work as a visual designer at an advertising agency. One day, the director of the sci-fi short film *REM* asked me to design the poster for his short. I realized that was what I had always wanted to do and that I could devote myself to it for real. A great movie needs a great poster. For me it is an essential piece, a window to the world created in the film that has to show the truth. And although I use computers as a tool, I try to give my works that handmade human touch that inspires and transcends a sheet of paper.

Sigourney
WEAVER
Felicity
JONES
Lewis
MACDOUGALL
Liam
NEESON
stories are wild creatures
A MONSTER CALLS
FROM J.A. BAYONA

2016
BEN AFFLECK HENRY CAVILL AMY ADAMS
JESSE EISENBERG DIANE LANE LAWRENCE FISHBURNE JEREMY IRONS HOLLY HUNTER GAL GADOT
BATMAN v SUPERMAN
DAWN OF JUSTICE

no one to trust   everyone to hate

THE 8TH FILM BY
QUENTIN TARANTINO

THE HATEFUL
EIGHT

SAMUEL L.   KURT   JENNIFER   WALTON
JACKSON   RUSSELL   JASON LEIGH   GOGGINS
DEMIAN   TIM   MICHAEL   and   BRUCE
BICHIR   ROTH   MADSEN   DERN

TRUTH
ALWAYS
FINDS
ITS WAY

A SHORT FILM BY JOSEBA ALFARO

DESTROY MADRID

DESTROYMADRID.COM

CAPTAIN AMERICA
THE WINTER SOLDIER

THE UNIVERSE KNEW WE WERE COMING

MAGELLAN

ARROWSTORM ENTERTAINMENT PRESENTS IN ASSOCIATION WITH FIRESPIRE PRODUCTIONS AND BOLD FILM PRODUCTIONS A FILM BY ROB YORK "MAGELLAN"
STARRING BRANDON RAY OLIVE K. DANOR GERALD WHITNEY PALMER NICOLA POSENER B.L. WALKER DAVEY MORRISON AND MATTHEW MERCER AS "FERDINAND"
MUSIC NATHANEL DREW EDITED ROB YORK PRODUCED ELLIOT YORK VISUAL CECIL B. COSTUME JOSEPH BELLISTON
EXECUTIVE JASON FALLER AND KYNAN GRIFFIN PRODUCED SCOTT BAIRD AND ROB YORK WRITTEN DIRECTED ROB YORK

FIRESPIRE   ARROWSTORM   BOLDFilms   #MAGELLANMOVIE
                                                    MAGELLANMOVIE

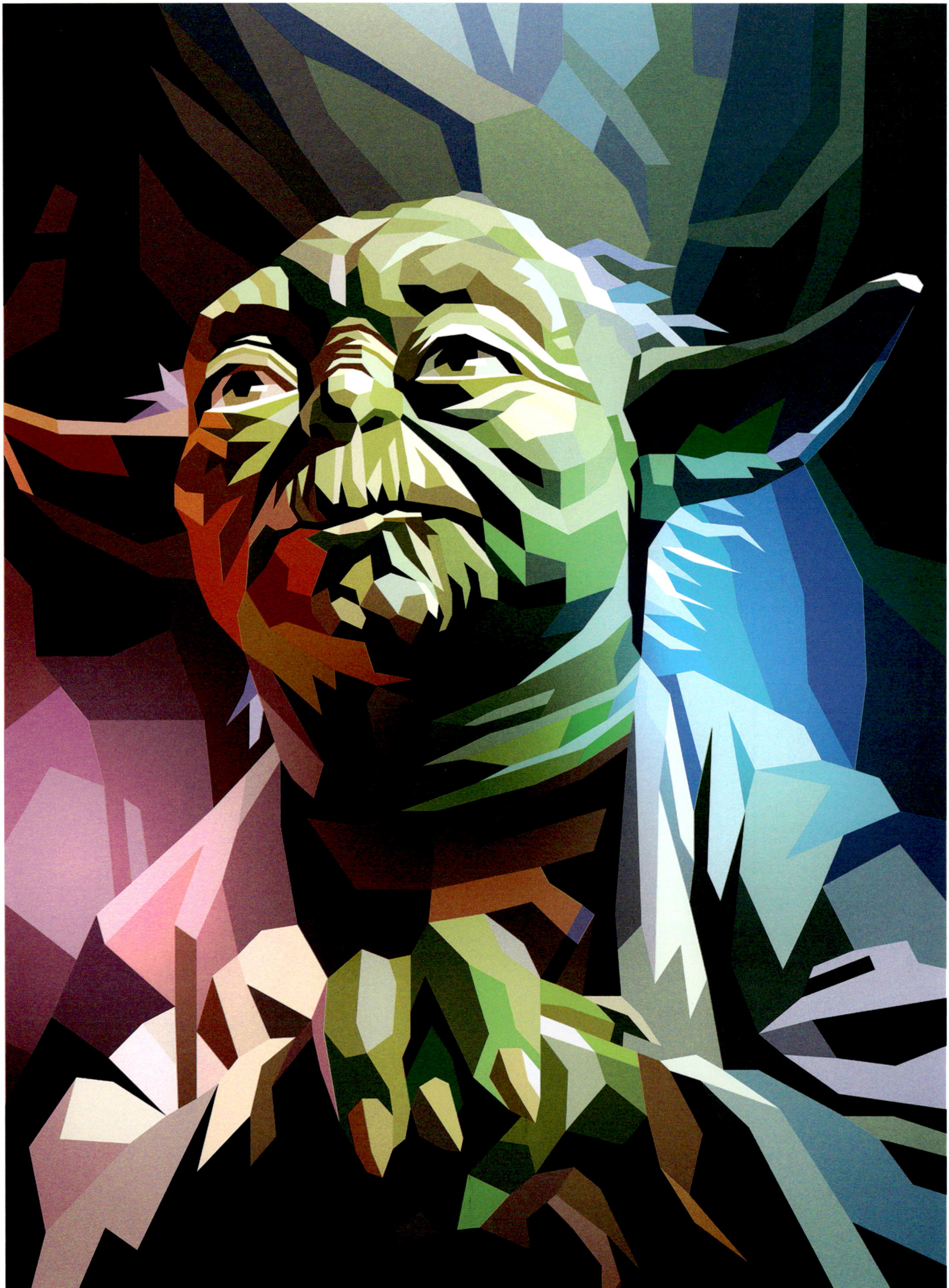

LIAM BRAZIER
www.liambrazier.com
www.posterspy.com/profile/liambrazier

Movies have always been amazing holidays away from myself, ninety-odd minute trips with friends and enemies I've never met to places alien or further reaching than the small seaside town I grew up in. Those visual stories do, and continue to, spark my imagination into wanting to praise that achievement, or prolong that enjoyment. I've always loved color and form, and that view of the world extends to the media I love to consume. Drawing tributes to these other pieces of art is meant as a humble hat tip, from my own perspective, in an attempt to showcase my admiration. I am drawn a lot of times to portraits as they play well in the style I work in, plus the characters are often iconic, and symbolic of the films they are featured in. The best movie posters surmise a plot, or a feeling, or a character into an image that is reminiscent of the film they enjoy. For me it's a selfish exercise, but it's always a great feeling to hear from someone else that something I've drawn has resonated with them.

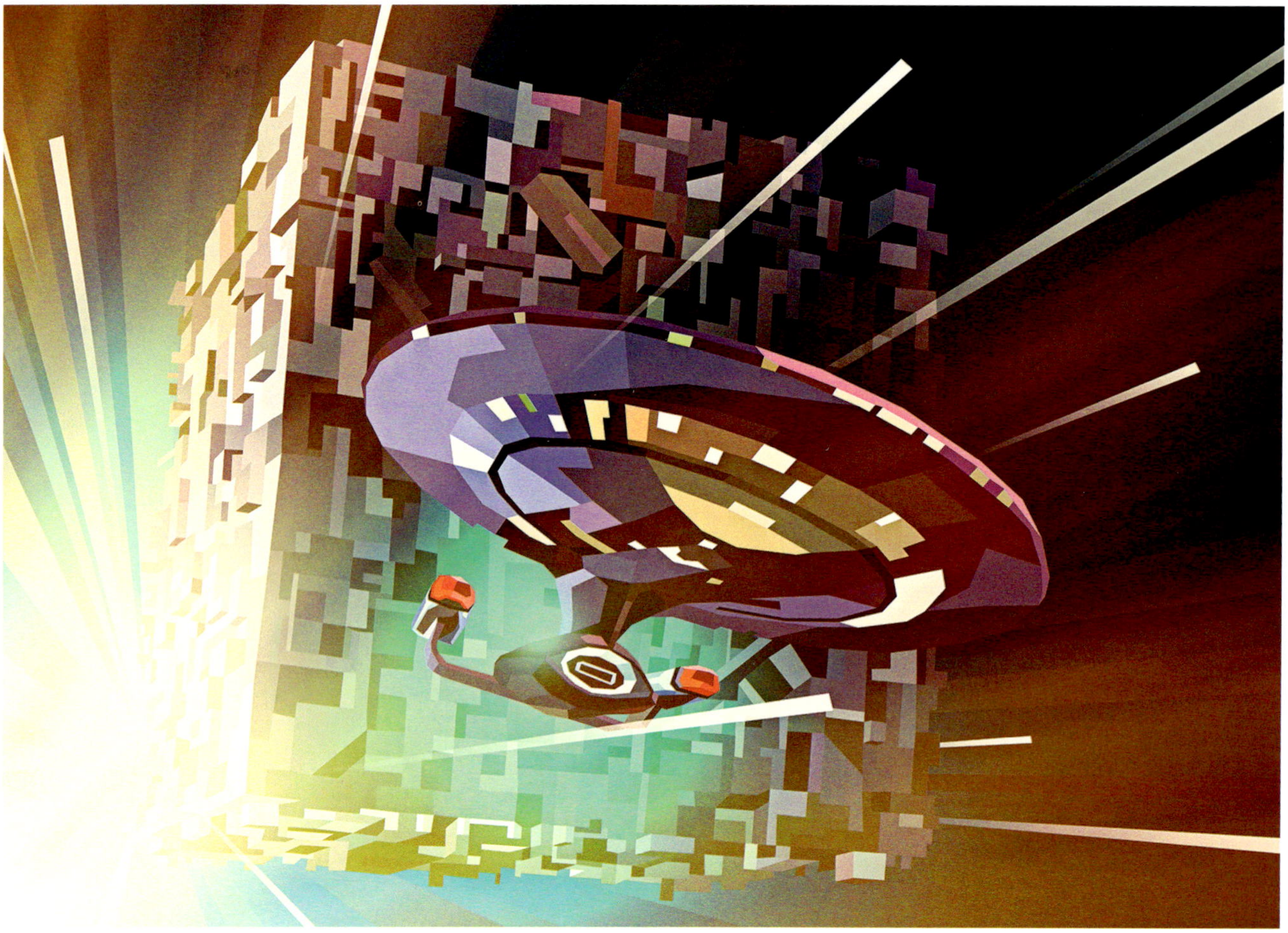

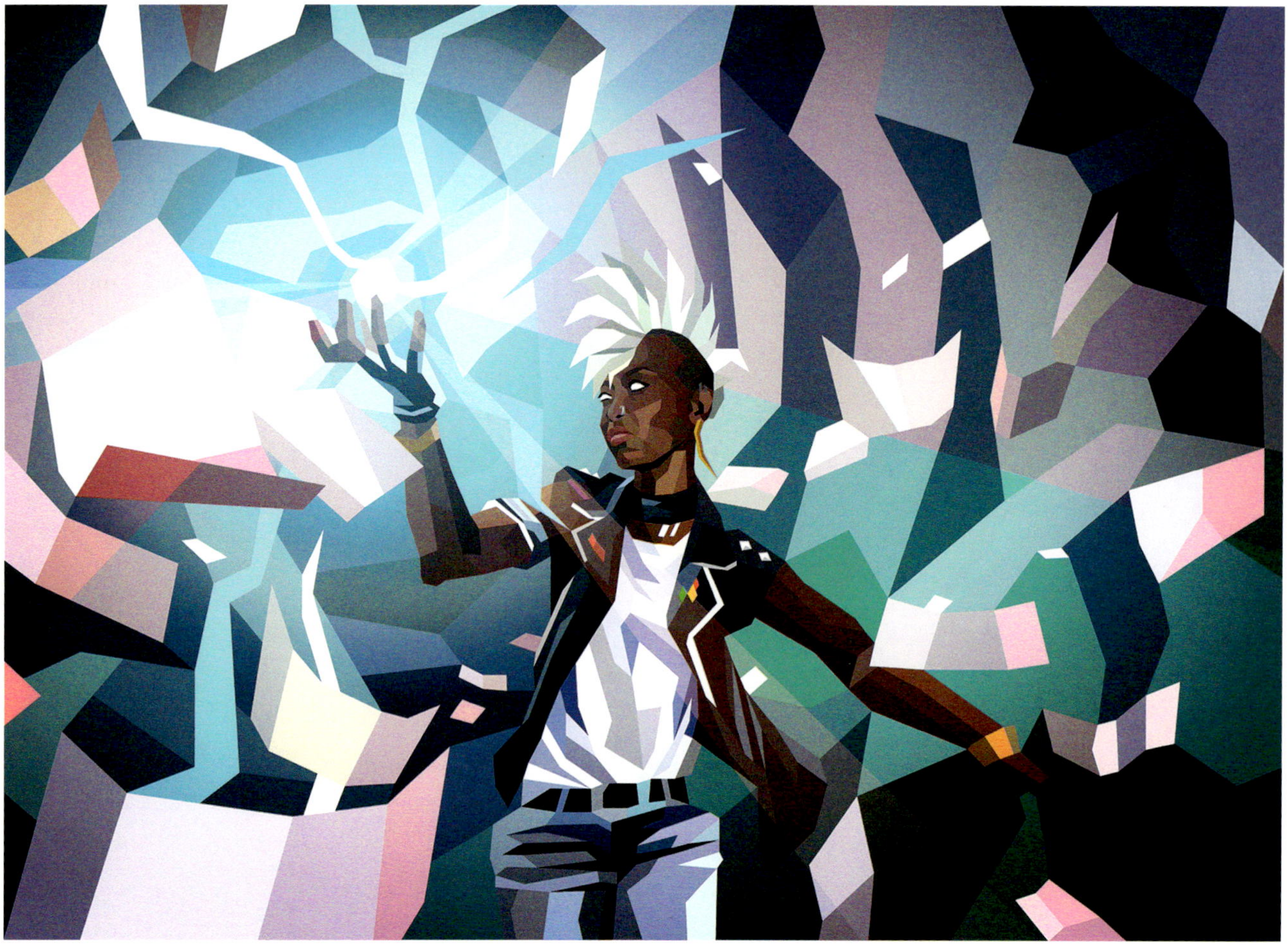

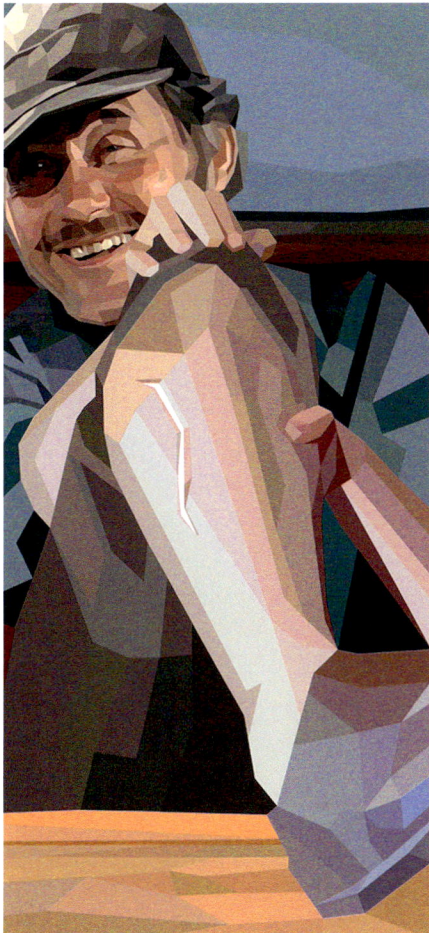

LIZA SHUMSKAYA
www.shumskayaart.tumblr.com
www.posterspy.com/profile/lizashumskaya

My passion with this particular artwork comes from my inner love for movies. I've been drawing my whole life. It's my hobby. So I decided to compile two things that I love the most—movies and drawing. Every time I watch a movie, I imagine a poster that will represent the idea of a movie in one small, silent piece of work. That will tell you a story without a single word. That will give a strong and correct idea of a movie for newcomers. I am so happy that my passion is slowly becoming my job. When I look at official movie posters, I see a team of professionals that worked hard and I'm always eager to test myself to see if I'm able to create something as extraordinary. I experimented with different styles and finally I found my own, the one I feel most comfortable with. You can see it in some of my works, a calm color palette and smooth lines.

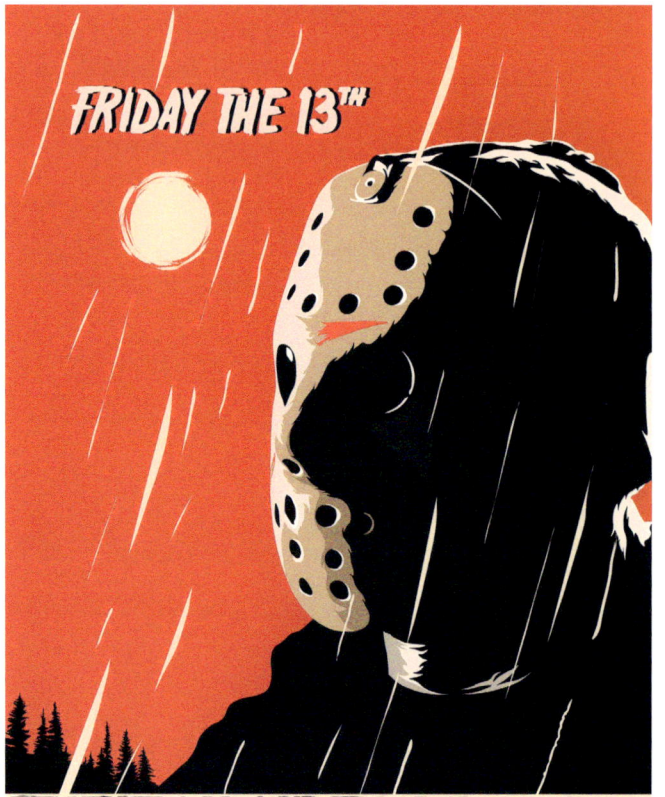

A TIM BURTON FILM

EDWARD SCISSORHANDS

TWENTIETH CENTURY FOX PRESENTS A TIM BURTON FILM. "EDWARD SCISSORHANDS" STARRING JOHNNY DEPP · WINONA RYDER · DIANNE WIEST · ANTHONY MICHAEL HALL
KATHY BAKER · VINCENT PRICE AS THE INVENTOR AND ALAN ARKIN MUSIC BY DANNY ELFMAN MAKEUP EFFECTS SUPERVISED BY STAN WINSTON EDITED BY RICHARD HALSEY, A.C.E.
PRODUCTION DESIGNER BO WELCH DIRECTOR OF PHOTOGRAPHY STEFAN CZAPSKY EXECUTIVE PRODUCER RICHARD HASHIMOTO STORY BY TIM BURTON AND CAROLINE THOMPSON
SCREENPLAY BY CAROLINE THOMPSON PRODUCED BY DENISE DI NOVI AND TIM BURTON DIRECTED BY TIM BURTON

LUKE BUTLAND
www.lostminddesignstudio.com
www.posterspy.com/profile/lost-mind

I'm a geek and I enjoy art, it's really that simple. I've loved film from a young age and pretty much used to live in Blockbuster. They say never judge a book by its cover, but I fully used to pick films on their cover art.

As I grew up so did my understanding of film poster art and how great key art can elevate a film and sometimes be better than the film itself. This love for film and art is really what led me into this fun little world of poster creation. Its just great to riff on a film you're excited about, or one from your past that you just love, and try to create something new and refreshing in your style.

SHHH...THEY WILL NEVER KNOW !!

DEADPOOL

A NEW CLASS OF HERO

GUARDIANS
OF
THE GALAXY

YOU'RE WELCOME

ROGER MOORE
AS
JAMES BOND 007
IN

THE MAN WITH THE
GOLDEN GUN

007

MAINGER
www.mainger.com
www.posterspy.com/profile/mainger

I started studying graphic arts and advertising in 2003 at Saint Luc Institute in Belgium. Then I worked in a communications agency in Paris and now I'm freelance. I've been absolutely fascinated by movies since I was a child. I frequently revisit film posters; there are so many possibilities. I'm especially inspired by action, adventure, sci-fi, and horror movies produced during the '80s and '90s from Carpenter to Spielberg. I also like working on typography, an important element to the poster's composition.

AXIS
BATMAN
WARNER BROS PRESENTS JACK NICHOLSON MICHAEL KEATON KIM BASINGER
A GUBER-PETERS COMPANY PRODUCTION A TIM BURTON FILM "BATMAN" ROBERT WUHL PAT HINGLE BILLY DEE WILLIAMS
MICHAEL GOUGH AND JACK PALANCE EDITOR RAY LOVEJOY PRODUCTION DESIGNED BY ANTON FURST
SONGS BY PRINCE MUSIC SCORE BY DANNY ELFMAN EXECUTIVE PRODUCERS BENJAMIN MELNIKER AND MICHAEL USLAN
CO-PRODUCER CHRIS KENNY BASED UPON BATMAN CHARACTERS CREATED BY BOB KANE AND PUBLISHED BY DC COMICS
STORY BY SAM HAMM SCREENPLAY BY SAM HAMM AND WARREN SKAAREN
PRODUCED BY JON PETERS & PETER GUBER DIRECTED BY TIM BURTON
SOUNDTRACK AVAILABLE ON WARNER BROS RECORDS CASSETTES AND CD

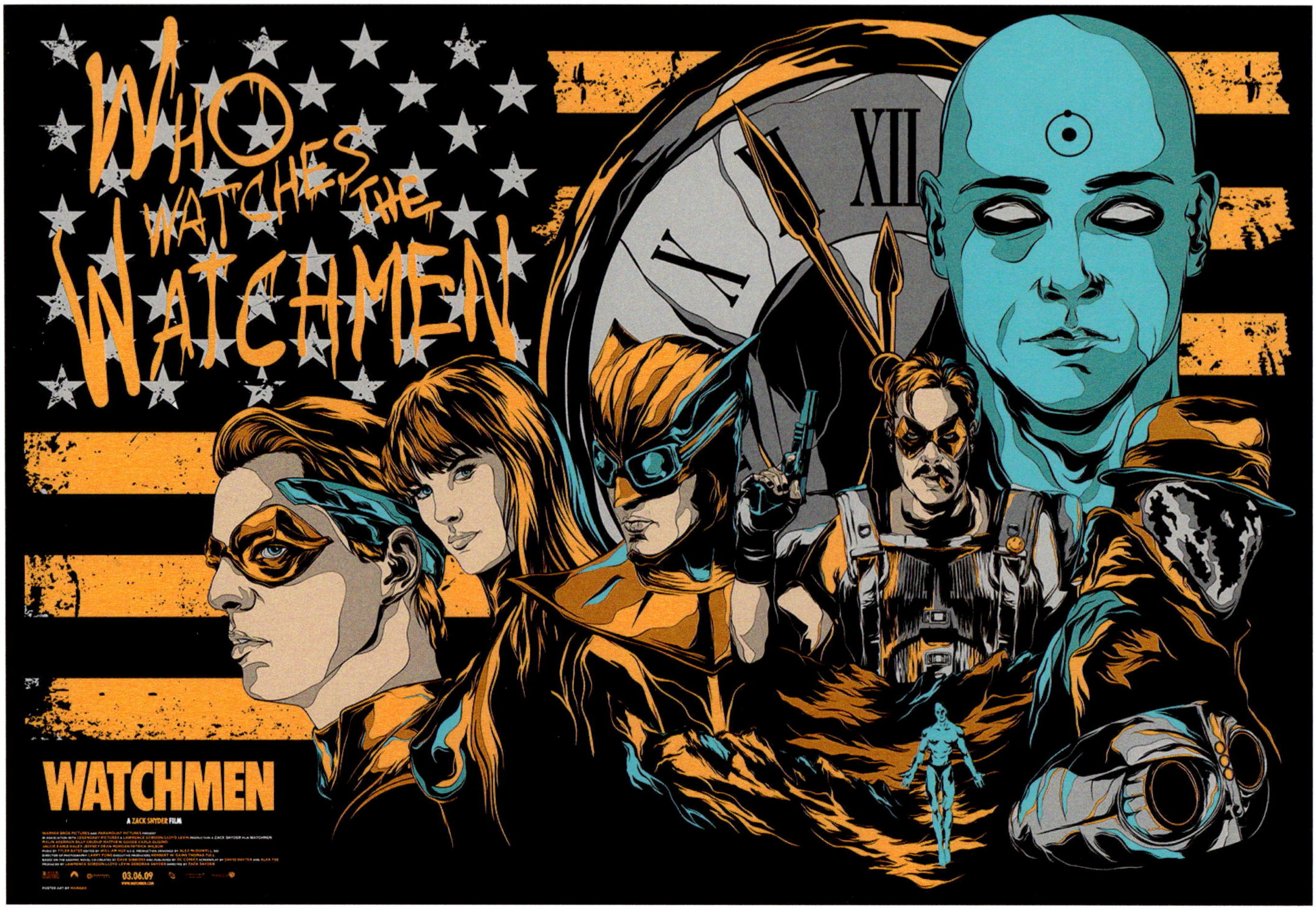
WHO WATCHES THE WATCHMEN
XII
X
WATCHMEN
A ZACK SNYDER FILM
03.06.09

スタジオジブリ作品
千と千尋の神隠し

POSTER ART BY MAINGER

Peter Pan

JAMES M. BARRIE

MARIA SUAREZ-INCLAN
www.msinclan.com
www.posterspy.com/profile/msinclan

SPOTLIGHT

Marcus Hamilton
HELL OR HIGH WATER

THE REVENANT
"I AIN'T AFRAID TO DIE ANYMORE,
I'D DONE IT ALREADY".

THE MARTIAN

BRIDGE OF SPIES

THE BIG SHORT

The Dude
THE BIG LEBOWSKI

Kevin Flynn
TRON

ROOM
"Hello Jack,
thanks for saving our little girl".

Brooklyn

MADMAX

Duane Jackson
THE LAST PICTURE SHOW

It's as simple as I love to draw and I love films. They get you to different worlds that you otherwise wouldn't be able to experience. When the movie is over you kind of want part of it to stay with you, and this nostalgic feeling can be fulfilled by movie posters. I guess it's my personal way to say, "Thank you for making this movie, I really enjoyed it."

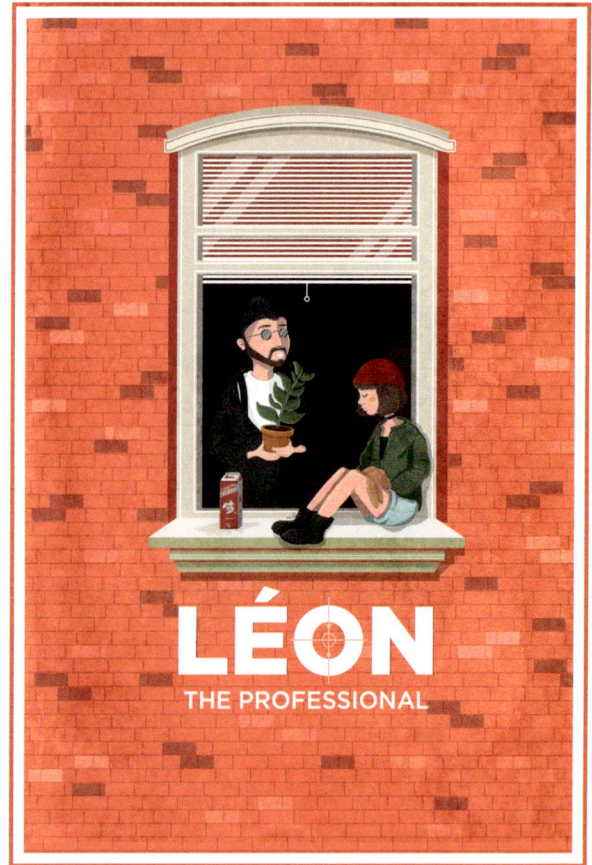

GOONIES

LÉON
THE PROFESSIONAL

WES ANDERSON

Bottle Rocket • Rushmore • The Royal Tenenbaums • The Life Aquatic • Hotel Chevalier • The Darjeeling Limited • Fantastic Mr. Fox • Moonrise Kingdom • The Grand Budapest Hotel

Expect the unexpected.
He does.
THE ADVENTURES OF
BUCKAROO
BANZAI
ACROSS THE 8TH DIMENSION

MATT GRIFFIN
www.mattgriffin.online
www.posterspy.com/profile/matthewjgriffin

Poster art is a special medium. Posters are your first glimpse into the world which they are advertising, they are the worm on the hook. Giving a taste of a wider story in just one image is the poster artist's challenge, and it's one we relish. Making a good poster is not just about taking some stills, Photoshopping them together, and throwing on some type (it's a shame that this is what some studios have relied upon in recent years). Thankfully artists like those in this book and on sites like PosterSpy are changing that. The movie poster as an art form is back.

For me personally, I love the process of distilling a film to one, iconic image. I'm also just as passionate about making type as images. Posters and Blu-ray covers allow me to design titles as well as the art—the perfect blend. I still can't quite believe it's what I do for a job.

MIRISCH PICTURES PRESENTS
"WEST SIDE STORY"
A ROBERT WISE PRODUCTION

STARRING NATALIE WOOD

RICHARD BEYMER RUSS TAMBLYN
RITA MORENO GEORGE CHAKIRIS

DIRECTED BY ROBERT WISE AND JEROME ROBBINS SCREENPLAY BY ERNEST LEHMAN
ASSOCIATE PRODUCER SAUL CHAPLIN CHOREOGRAPHY BY JEROME ROBBINS
MUSIC BY LEONARD BERNSTEIN LYRICS BY STEPHEN SONDHEIM
BASED UPON THE STAGE PLAY PRODUCED BY ROBERT E. GRIFFITH AND HAROLD S. PRINCE
BOOK BY ARTHUR LAURENTS

WEST SIDE STORY

MATT NEEDLE
www.mattneedle.co.uk
www.posterspy.com/profile/needledesign

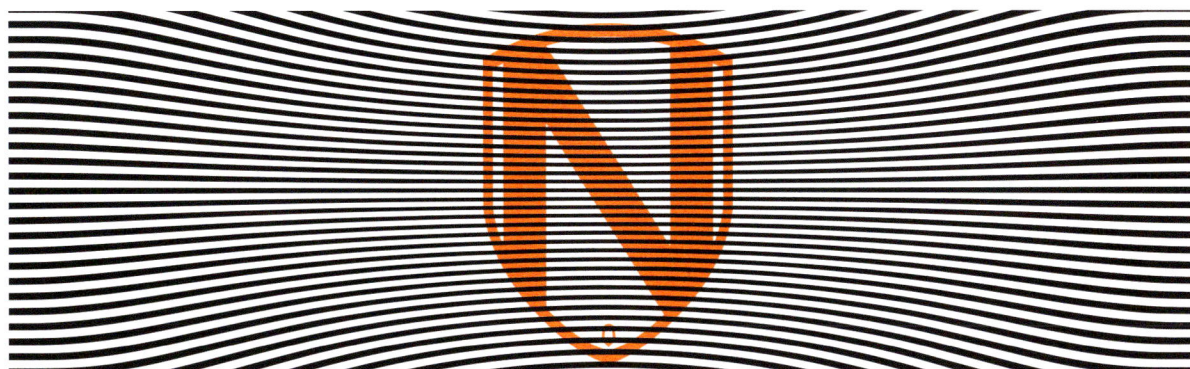

Film posters have inspired me from a very early age. I remember as a child being enamored with the work of Drew Struzan (long before I ever knew who he was). I collected posters and VHS covers in a scrapbook and redrew my own versions. Later on in my younger years, I discovered the work of Saul Bass through my love of Hitchcock films, and from there I knew I wanted to create and make stuff as a job when I grew up. Through Bass I was introduced to the world of graphic design and illustration, and fell in love with the subject. When I finished school I went to college and then uni to study design and illustration. Almost all of my projects had a film influence or twist.

Enchantment Under
The Sea Dance

COFFEE   SANDWICHES   SODA

LOU'S
CAFE

NOV   12   1955

EX MACHINA

DIRECTED BY ALEX GARLAND

ALICIA VIKANDER
DOMHNALL GLEESON
OSCAR ISAAC

WILLIAM PETER BLATTY'S THE EXORCIST
DIRECTED BY WILLIAM FRIEDKIN

STARRING ELLEN BURSTYN • MAX VON SYDOW • LEE J. COBB
KITTY WINN • JACK MACGOWRAN
JASON MILLER AS FATHER KARRAS LINDA BLAIR AS REGAN
PRODUCED BY WILLIAM PETER BLATTY EXECUTIVE PRODUCER NOEL MARSHALL
SCREENPLAY BY WILLIAM PETER BLATTY BASED ON HIS NOVEL
FROM WARNER BROS. Ⓦ A WARNER COMMUNICATIONS COMPANY

R RESTRICTED
UNDER 17 REQUIRES ACCOMPANYING
PARENT OR ADULT GUARDIAN

MATT TALBOT
www.mattrobot.com
www.posterspy.com/profile/mattrobot

Making a movie poster is like putting together a puzzle, but there are a million ways that the pieces can be put back together. Should I depict a scene from the movie? Is there an abstract way to capture the feeling I got from watching? Will a simple portrait of the star say enough? There's no wrong answer; no wrong approach. To me, that's why posters are so exciting to design. I love the challenge of trying to find a detail, a theme—some kind of angle that says something new about a movie. Shake up the pieces, lay them out, and see what kind of picture can be put together. Every poster is a new chance to do something different—and hopefully something great—in service to a film.

BE NICE.
UNTIL IT'S TIME
TO NOT BE NICE.

ROAD HOUSE

UNITED ARTISTS PRESENTS
A SILVER PICTURES PRODUCTION PATRICK SWAYZE "ROAD HOUSE"
BEN GAZZARA KELLY LYNCH AND SAM ELLIOTT FEATURED MUSICAL PERFORMANCE BY THE JEFF HEALEY BAND
EXECUTIVE PRODUCERS STEVE PERRY AND TIM MOORE STORY BY DAVID LEE HENRY SCREENPLAY BY DAVID LEE HENRY AND HILARY HENKIN
PRODUCED BY JOEL SILVER DIRECTED BY ROWDY HERRINGTON
POSTER BY MATT TALBOT | MATTTALBOT.COM

CHARLIZE THERON IS

FuRioSa

IN
MAD MAX
FURY ROAD

WARNER BROS. PICTURES PRESENTS
IN ASSOCIATION WITH VILLAGE ROADSHOW PICTURES
A KENNEDY MILLER MITCHELL PRODUCTION A GEORGE MILLER FILM "MAD MAX: FURY ROAD"
TOM HARDY CHARLIZE THERON NICHOLAS HOULT HUGH KEAYS-BYRNE
ROSIE HUNTINGTON-WHITELEY RILEY KEOUGH ZOE KRAVITZ ABBEY LEE COURTNEY EATON
EDITED BY MARGARET SIXEL PRODUCTION DESIGN BY COLIN GIBSON CINEMATOGRAPHY BY JOHN SEALE
EXECUTIVE PRODUCERS IAN SMITH GRAHAM BURKE BRUCE BERMAN
WRITTEN BY GEORGE MILLER BRENDAN MCCARTHY NICK LATHOURIS
PRODUCED BY DOUG MITCHELL GEORGE MILLER P.J. VOETEN DIRECTED BY GEORGE MILLER

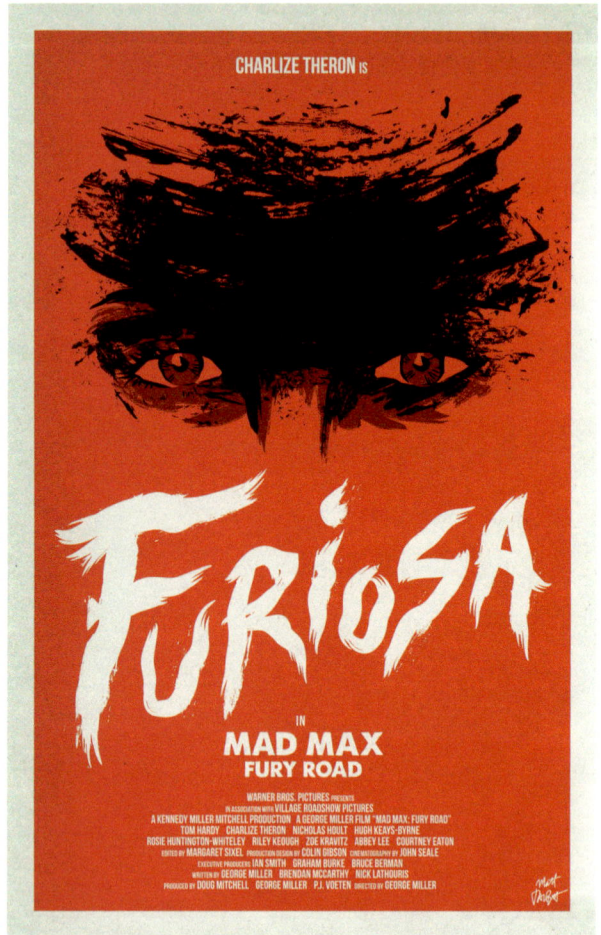

FROM EDGAR WRIGHT, DIRECTOR OF SHAUN OF THE DEAD AND HOT FUZZ

SIMON PEGG
NICK FROST

THE WORLD'S END

WITH PADDY CONSIDINE MARTIN FREEMAN EDDIE MARSAN ROSAMUND PIKE

WRITTEN BY SIMON PEGG & EDGAR WRIGHT DIRECTED BY EDGAR WRIGHT

PRESENTED BY UNIVERSAL PICTURES IN ASSOCIATION WITH RELATIVITY MEDIA A WORKING TITLE PRODUCTION IN ASSOCIATION WITH BIG TALK PICTURES

THE SHINING

A STANLEY KUBRICK FILM
STARRING JACK NICHOLSON SHELLEY DUVALL "THE SHINING" WITH SCATMAN CROTHERS DANNY LLOYD
BASED ON THE NOVEL BY STEPHEN KING SCREENPLAY BY STANLEY KUBRICK & DIANE JOHNSON PRODUCED AND DIRECTED BY STANLEY KUBRICK EXECUTIVE PRODUCER JAN HARLAN
POSTER MATTTALBOT.COM

ALL-BRAND-NEW!
NEVER SEEN ON TV!
MADE IN SPECTACULAR COLOR

A WILLIAM DOZIER PRODUCTION
ADAM WEST · BURT WARD
BATMAN

FEATURING A GALLERY OF DASTARDLY VILLAINS
LEE MERIWETHER AS CATWOMAN   CESAR ROMERO AS THE JOKER
BURGESS MEREDITH AS THE PENGUIN   FRANK GORSHIN AS THE RIDDLER
PRODUCED BY WILLIAM DOZIER   DIRECTED BY LESLIE H. MARTINSON
WRITTEN BY LORENZO SEMPLE, JR.   COLOR BY DE LUXE

PG PARENTAL GUIDANCE SUGGESTED
SOME MATERIAL MAY NOT BE SUITABLE FOR CHILDREN

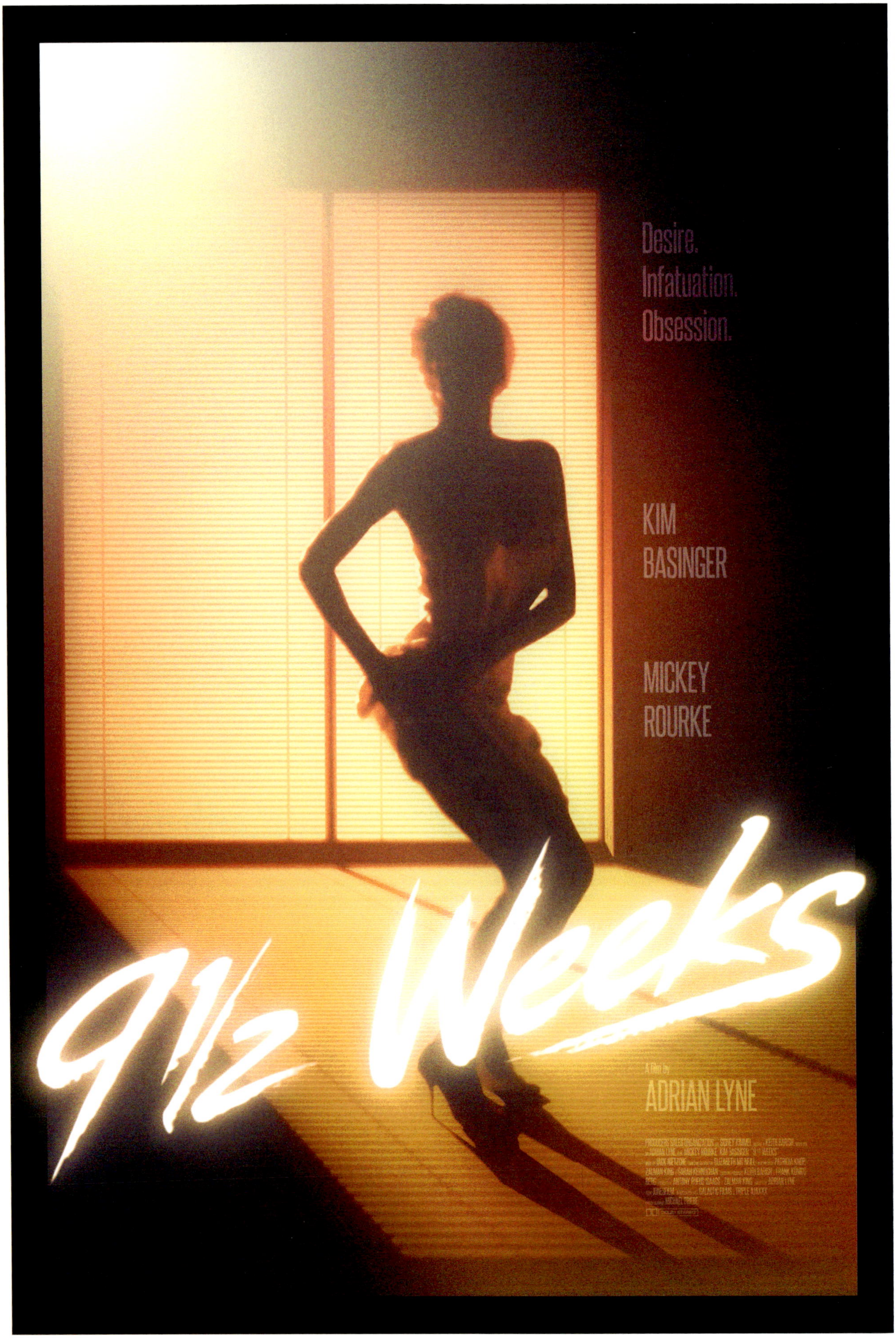

Desire.
Infatuation.
Obsession.

KIM
BASINGER

MICKEY
ROURKE

9½ Weeks

A Film by
ADRIAN LYNE

MICHAEL FRIEBE
www.posterspy.com/profile/raborlatte

I think the first time I remember experiencing a movie poster was when I first saw John Alvin's artwork for *E.T.* as a child. There were many things that struck me about it. For one, it was referencing *The Creation of Adam*, which even as a child I, surprisingly, was familiar with. Also, I realized the narrative element movie posters convey. This obviously was a story transcending beyond the boundaries of Earth, it is about the friendly relationship of an alien creature and a boy and there is a lot of mystery to be expected. All of that became apparent within the blink of an eye. Having worked at a video rental store for many years while studying design, my understanding of movie posters grew beyond seeing them as pure marketing instruments, but as an integral part of the entire art form that movies represent. The right or wrong artwork can determine a movie's fate, influence what people think of it (without having seen a single second of said film), and guide how people feel about watching it at all. And this is exactly how I approach designing movie posters as well. What do I want people to feel? What do I want people to think? What do I want to tell my audience this movie is about, without giving it all away?

ANDRÉ
BENJAMIN

HAYLEY
ATWELL

IMOGEN
POOTS

JIMI
ALL IS BY MY SIDE

DRIVE
FILMDISTRICT PRESENTS IN ASSOCIATION WITH BOLD FILMS AND ODDLOT ENTERTAINMENT A MARC PLATT/MOTEL MOVIES PRODUCTION A NICOLAS WINDING REFN FILM
RYAN GOSLING "DRIVE" CAREY MULLIGAN BRYAN CRANSTON CHRISTINA HENDRICKS RON PERLMAN WITH OSCAR ISAAC AND ALBERT BROOKS
MINDY MARIN, C.S.A. ERIN BENACH CLIFF MARTINEZ BETH MICKLE MAT NEWMAN NEWTON THOMAS SIGEL, A.S.C.
DAVID LANCASTER GARY MICHAEL WALTERS BILL LISCHAK LINDA McDONOUGH JEFFREY STOTT PETER SCHLESSEL
MARC PLATT ADAM SIEGEL GIGI PRITZKER MICHEL LITVAK JOHN PALERMO JAMES SALLIS HOSSEIN AMINI NICOLAS WINDING REFN
R RESTRICTED
FILMDISTRICT

MICHAEL GAMBRIEL
www.mikegambriel.com
www.posterspy.com/profile/mike-gambriel

I've loved watching films and drawing from an early age, especially when growing up in a small seaside town with not much else to do!

My earliest memory of film poster art was of course from the great Drew Struzan, with his *Indiana Jones* and *Star Wars* posters amongst many others. I think every film poster artist owes something to his work. I've only recently started making my own alternative film posters and I'm loving every minute of it! I'm a freelance illustrator by trade, specializing in portrait and figural work, so along with loving film, creating alternative film poster designs is a natural progress I guess. Even though film poster art isn't in such high demand as in Drew's day, I'll keep producing them as I love to do so. Who knows? I might get commissioned to produce one someday!

IRON MAN

POINT
BREAK

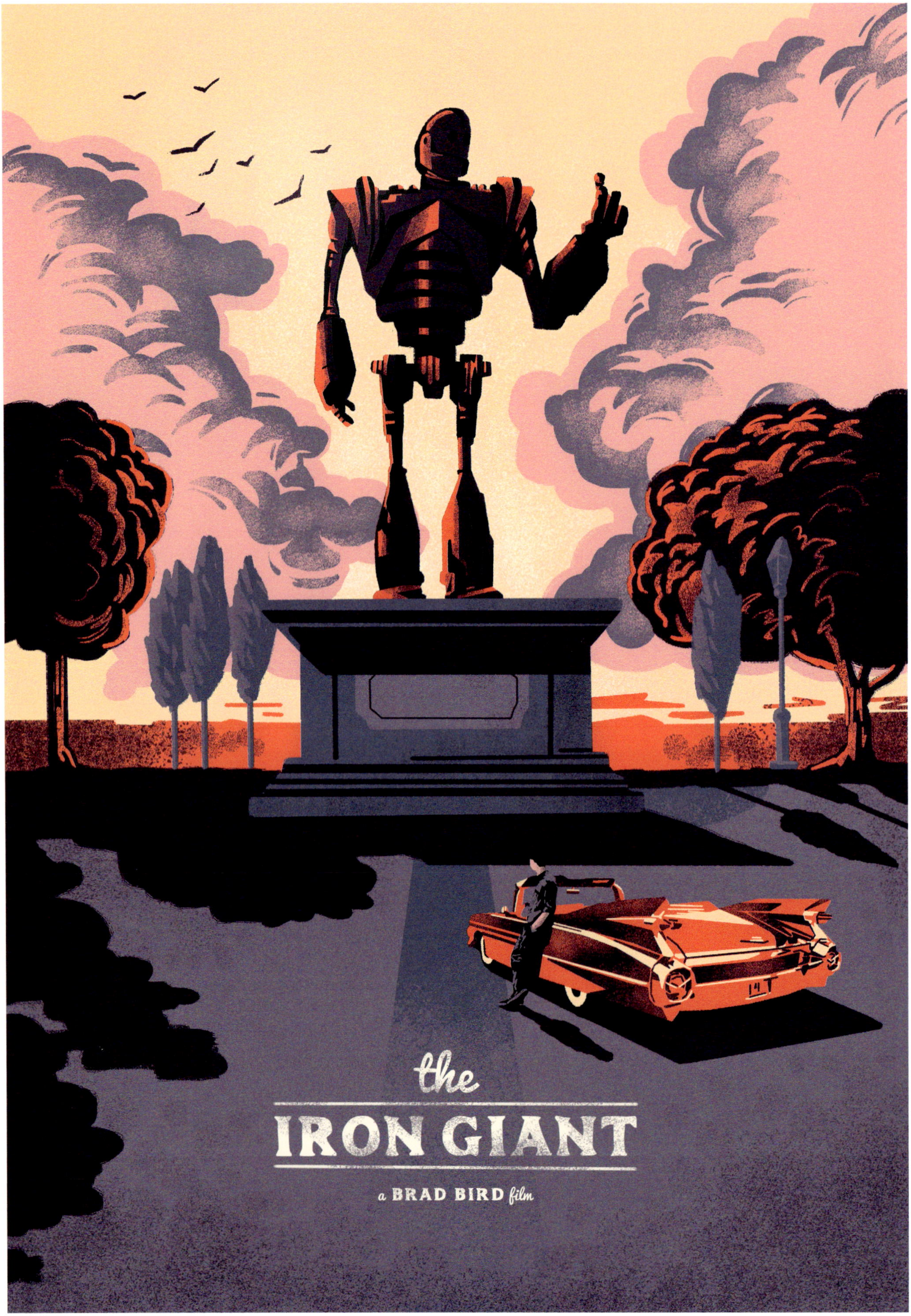
the
IRON GIANT
a BRAD BIRD film

MOBOKEH
www.mobokeh.com
www.posterspy.com/profile/mobokeh

As a graphic designer by trade, I turned to illustration for personal projects as a way of having a creative outlet and to focus on developing my skills with visual compositions. It's appealing to me to create content on subject matters that I love. I get to express my particular interpretation of the scenes I want to explore. I love how movie posters can get across subtle hints, tones, and elements of the story, without giving too much away. With my own work, I started developing more elaborate compositions in the form of movie poster artworks, and explored typographic elements in some of my pieces, which hopefully feeds back into my design work!

BATMAN v SUPERMAN
DAWN OF JUSTICE

THE
WALK
JOSEPH GORDON-LEVITT

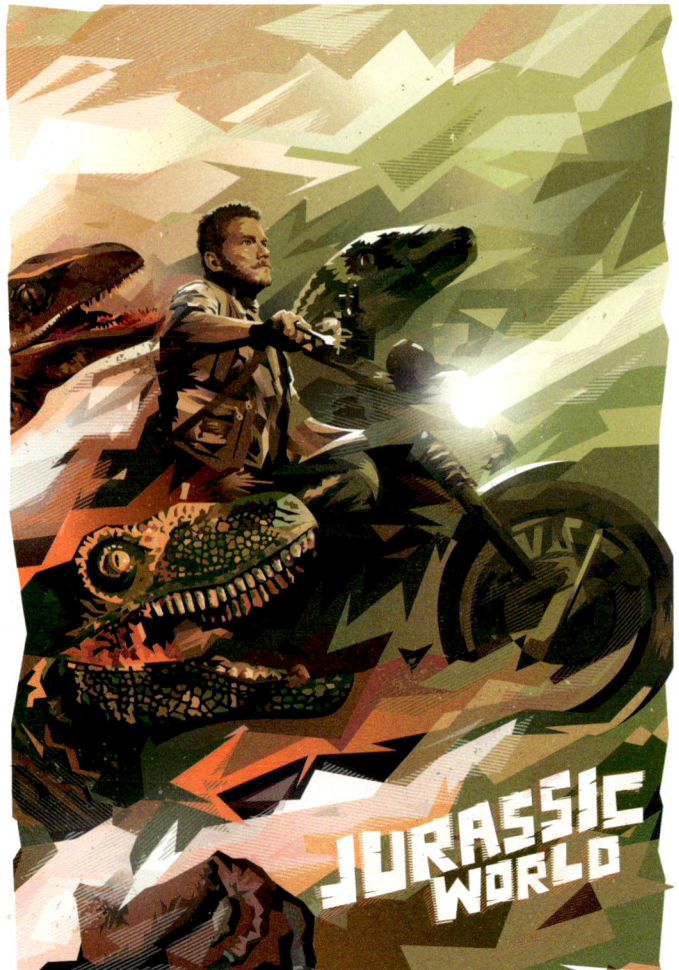

JURASSIC
WORLD

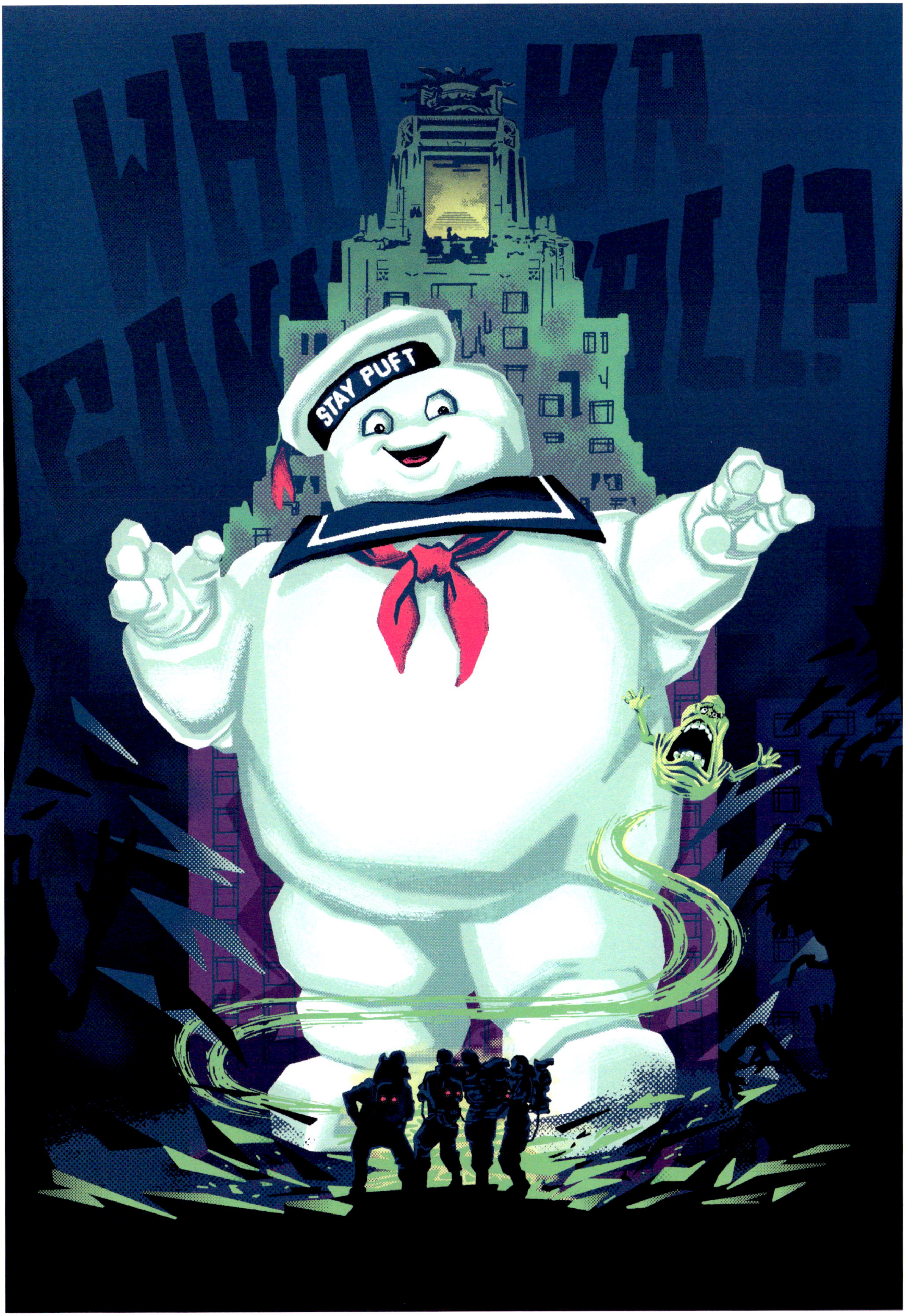
WHO YA
STAY PUFT

CAROL REED'S
THE THIRD MAN

JOSEPH COTTEN
ALIDA VALLI
ORSON WELLES
TREVOR HOWARD

"A BRITISH
MOVIE MASTERPIECE"

Neil Davies Illustration

NEIL DAVIES
www.neildaviesillustration.co.uk
www.posterspy.com/profile/neil-davies

I've been a freelance illustrator for a little while now, most of my work being caricature. It's only recently I've started producing poster art. It's been inspiring to see the amount and quality of work already out there in the poster art community. My work is almost all digital, so I spent some time finding my way to create the type of poster art I like in that medium. My biggest inspiration is, like many, Drew Struzan. There really is no one better. His *Indiana Jones and the Last Crusade* painting is still my favorite poster ever. It's really exciting to see lots of current artists producing stunning poster art with the same life and energy but digitally, something that I didn't think was really possible until recently. I'm having lots of fun exploring ways to do just that. I don't want to get tied to a computer screen though, so I recently painted a poster for *Star Wars: The Force Awakens* on 30" x 40" illustration board with acrylics and colored pencils—my first poster produced that way. I'm really happy with how it turned out and I'm very excited to produce more poster art both traditionally and digitally in the future!

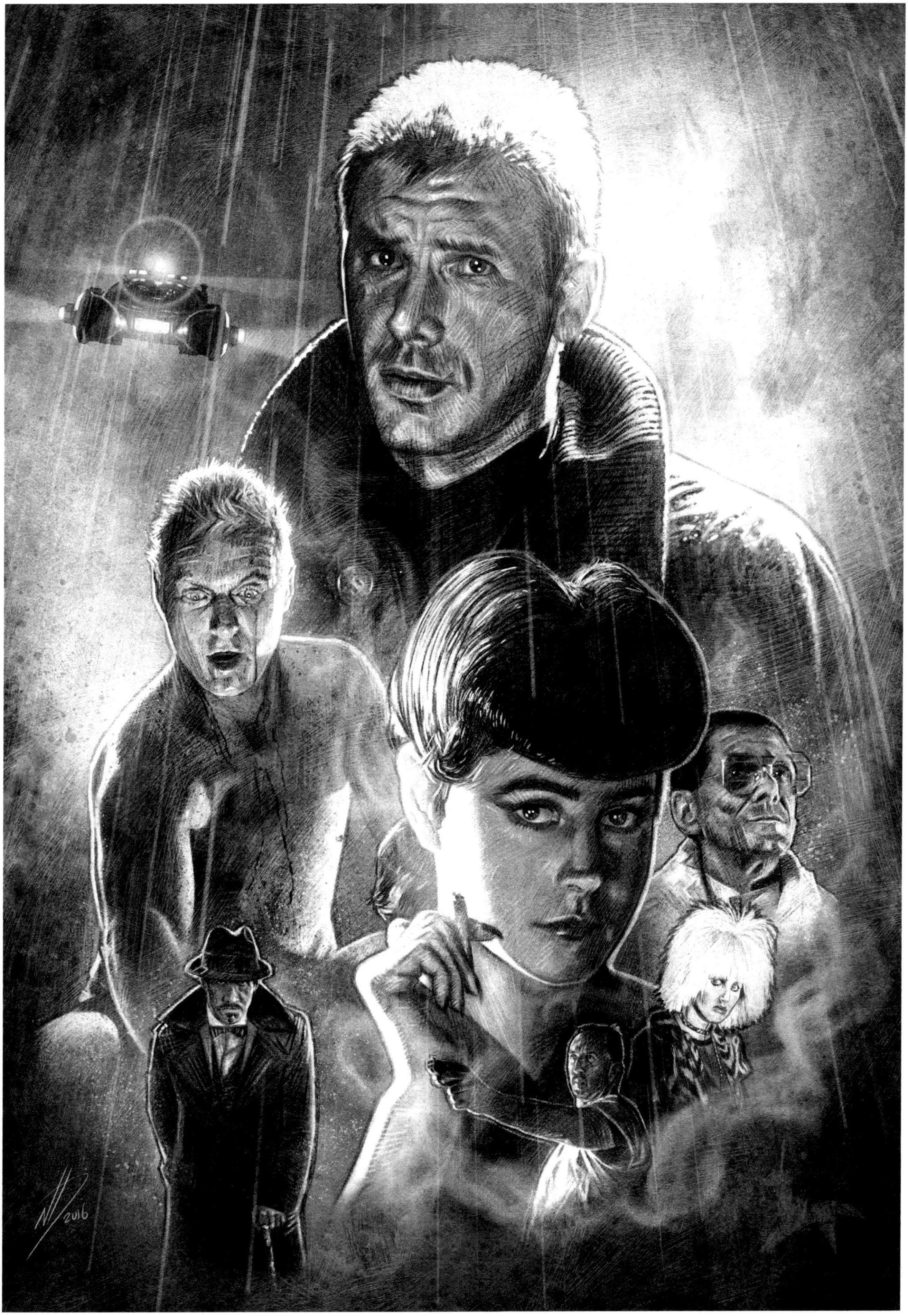
2016

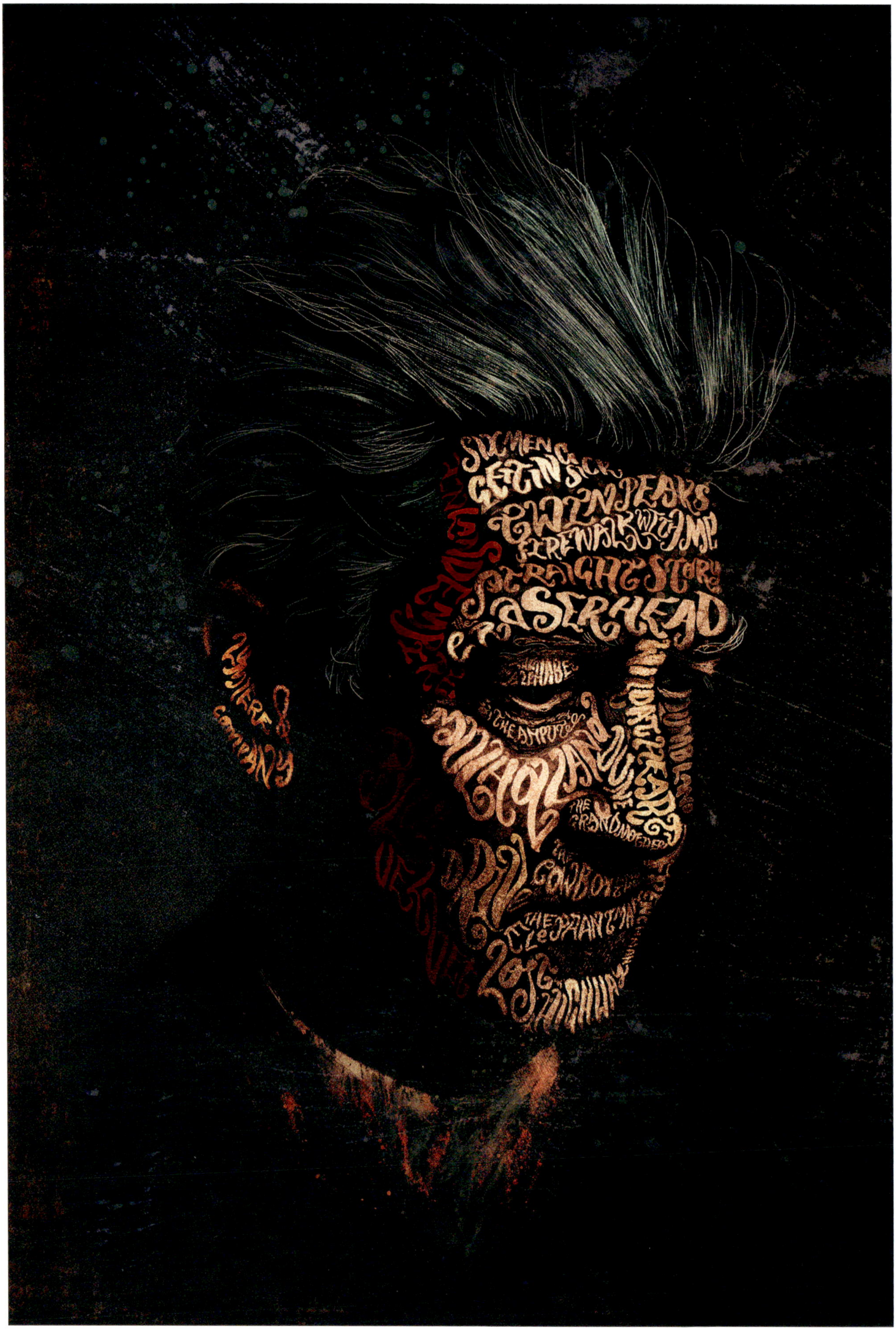
TWIN PEAKS
FIRE WALK WITH ME
STRAIGHT STORY
ERASERHEAD
THE COWBOY

PETER STRAIN
www.peterstrain.co.uk
www.posterspy.com/profile/peter-strain

When I first left university I wasn't sure what direction to take my illustration work, so I initially designed film posters as a way to develop my style. I've always loved and been inspired by film so it made sense to try to harness that passion for one medium and put it into another. I really like the challenge of trying to reinvent well known iconography and turn it into something new.

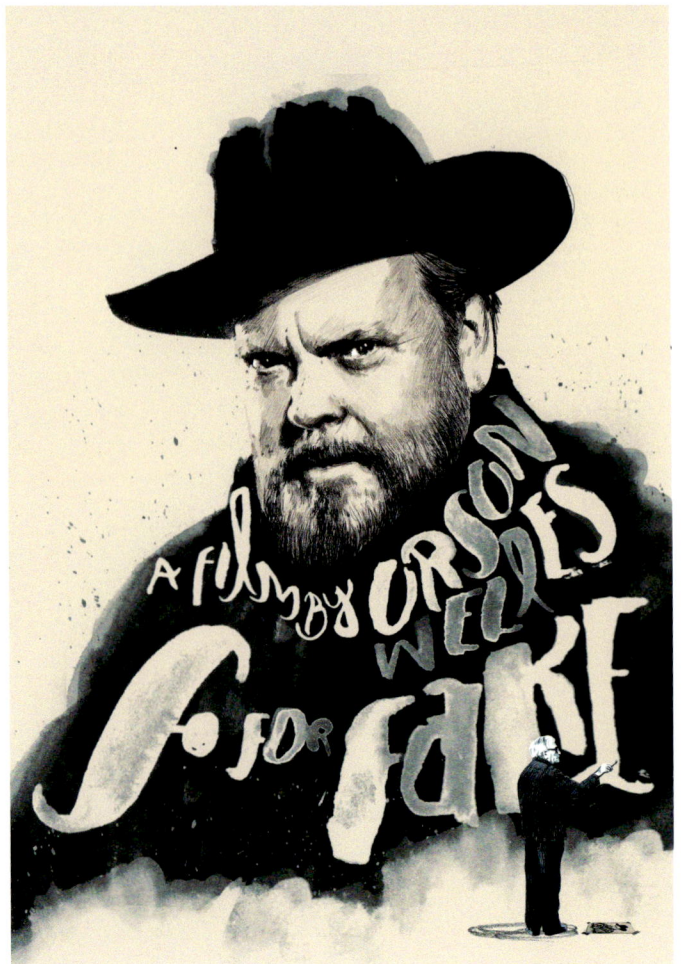

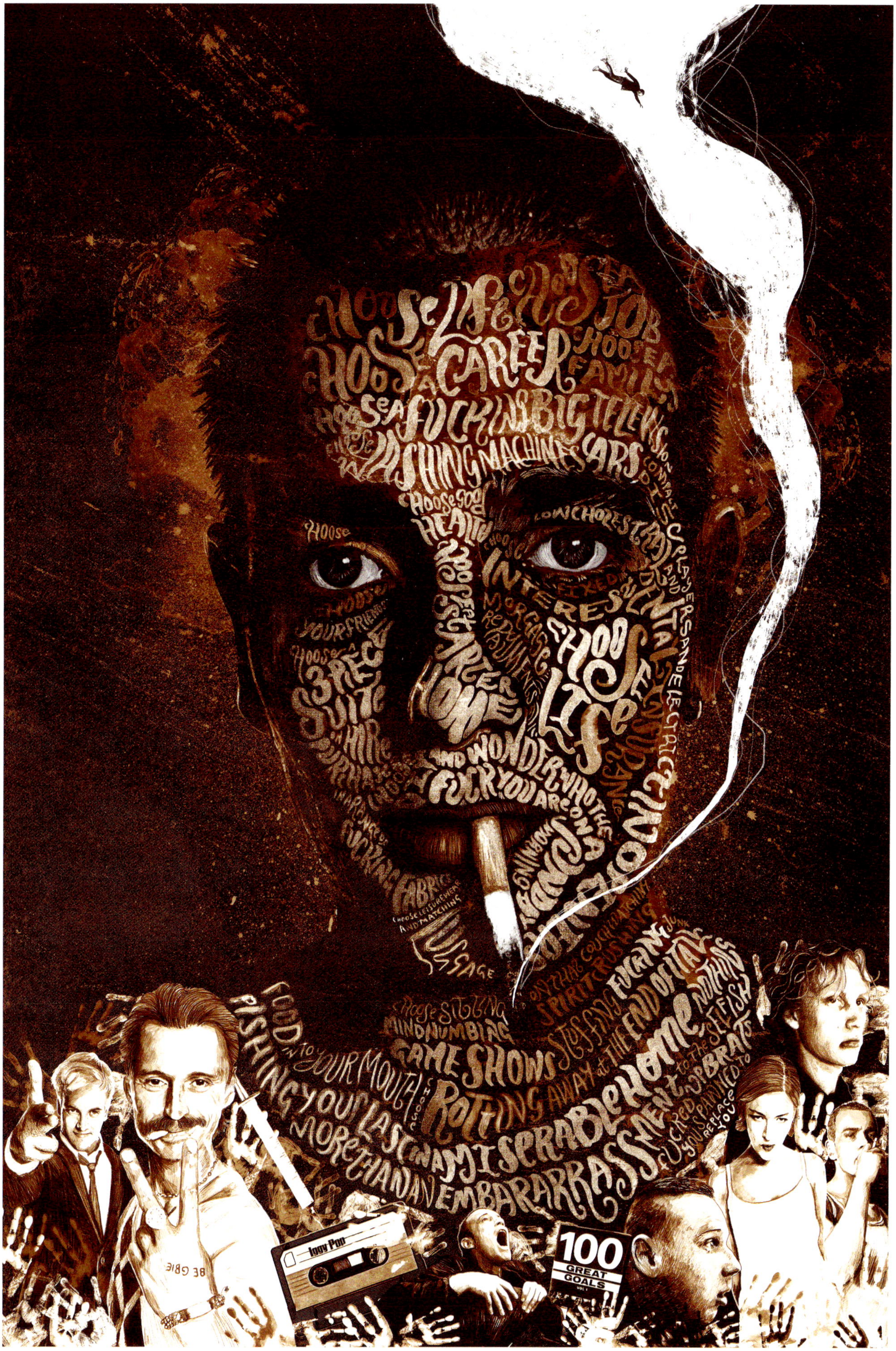
Iggy Pop
100 GREAT GOALS

THX 1138

THE FUTURE IS HERE

RAFAL ROLA
www.rafalrola.pl
www.posterspy.com/profile/rafalrola

Movies have always been a part of my life, so it is natural that they are also part of my creations. I especially like science fiction movies from the '80s. Designing new and interesting work is a real challenge, so I mostly choose movies that have really made an impression on me. I like to paint portraits. People are the most important in movies so my work is based on characters and faces.

THE
INFILTRATOR

ROGUE
ONE

TWENTIETH CENTURY FOX PRESENTS

ALIEN

THE REVENANT

BATMAN

NEVER GIVE UP, NEVER SURRENDER!

GalaxyQuest

DREAMWORKS PICTURES PRESENT A MARK JOHNSON PRODUCTION "GALAXY QUEST" TIM ALLEN SIGOURNEY WEAVER ALAN RICKMAN
TONY SHALHOUB SAM ROCKWELL DARYL MITCHELL CO-PRODUCERS SUZANN ELLIS AND SONA GOURGOURIS MUSIC BY DAVID NEWMAN ALIEN MAKE UP AND CREATURES BY STAN WINSTON
COSTUME DESIGNER ALBERT WOLSKY EDITED BY DON ZIMMERMAN A.C.E. PRODUCTION DESIGNER LINDA DESCENNA DIRECTOR OF PHOTOGRAPHY JERZY ZIELINSKI EXECUTIVE PRODUCER ELIZABETH CANTILLON
PRODUCED BY MARK JOHNSON CHARLES NEWIRTH STORY BY DAVID HOWARD SCREENPLAY BY DAVID HOWARD AND ROBERT GORDON DIRECTED BY DEAN PARISOT

RICH DAVIES

www.turksworks.co.uk
www.posterspy.com/profile/turksworks

I've had a passion for movie posters since I was a young child. I was fortunate enough to grow up in the 1980s, and being a huge movie fan, the posters were a window into the film before you even saw the movie. The hand-painted posters by the likes of Drew Struzan, John Alvin, Richard Amsel, and Brian Bysouth gave you a taster of the film in a single image. In some cases they were better than the films themselves! My bedroom walls were covered with these posters, usually obtained from my local video shop during the VHS boom of the '80s. Naturally, this fascination with the poster has stayed with me throughout my career in design and particularly now as a freelance illustrator. I always use these great masters of the movie poster as an inspiration and try to use color, tone, and layout to create a snapshot of the movie in one image like they did with such great success. In a way, I'm doing just what I did when I was a kid with pencil and paper and creating my own take on movies that are very special to me. It's this fusion of all things I love—art and movies—which means so much to me. It's not just a nostalgia trip either, I'm fortunate enough to do it for a living now, too. So it's come full circle.

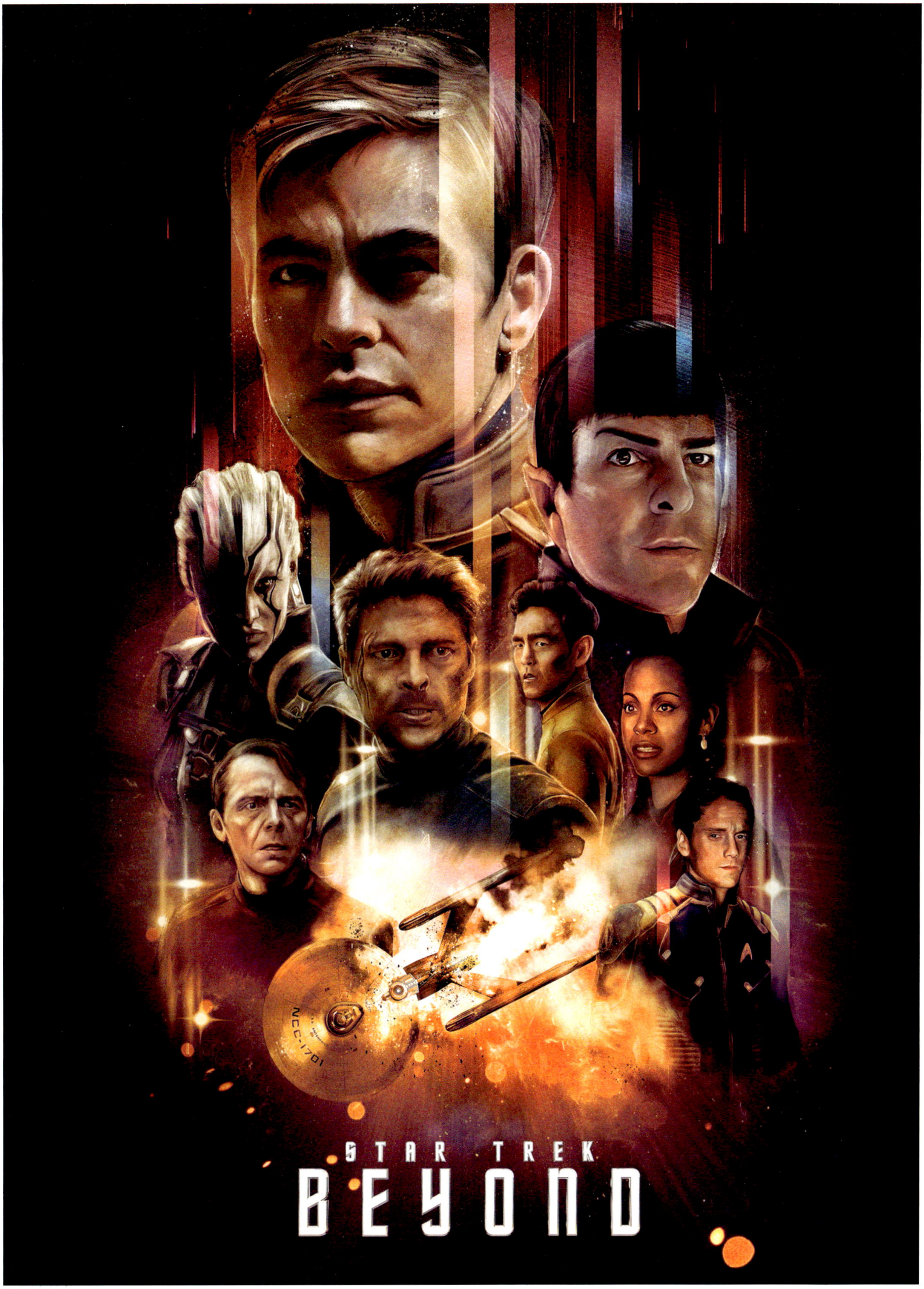
NCC-1701
STAR TREK
BEYOND

ROBERT LOCKLEY
www.posterspy.com/profile/rlockley

For me, creating alternative movie posters is purely a love thing. The work I produce is never for financial or critical gain, but out of respect and affection for the source material. To be a part of that world, to put your own spin on something so cherished, so beloved the world over is about as good as it gets. The rise of the alternative movie poster community through collectives such as Mondo, Poster Posse, and PosterSpy offers a shared appreciation that itself spawns creativity.

IN SPACE NO ONE CAN HEAR YOU

SCREAM

TOM SKERRITT VERONICA CARTRIGHT YAPHET KOTTO JOHN HURT IAN HOLM HARRY DEAN
STANTON AND SIGOURNEY WEAVER IN A RIDLEY SCOTT FILM @TWENTIETH CENTURY FOX

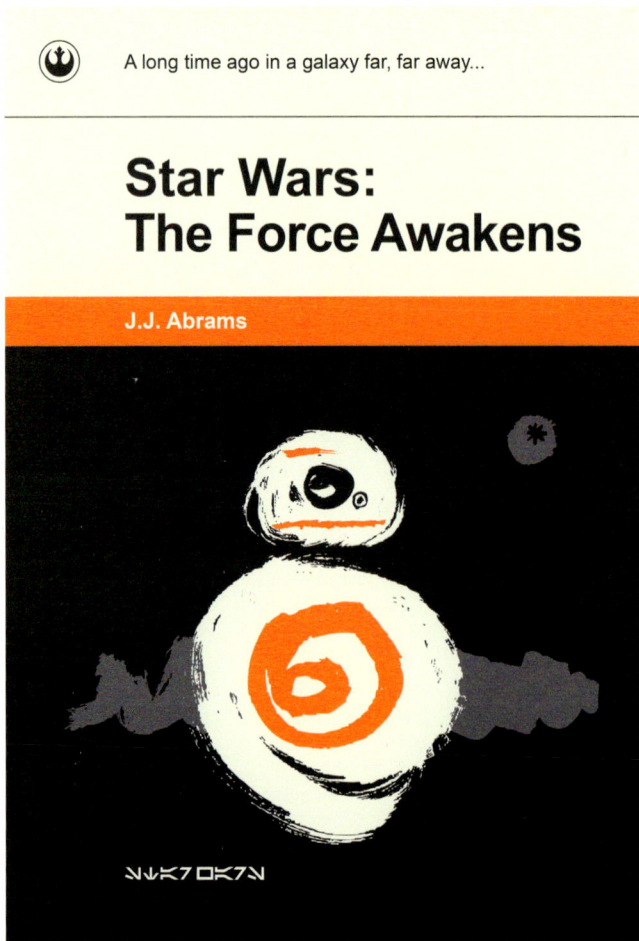

MARVEL

A long time ago in a galaxy far, far away...

Star Wars:
The Force Awakens

J.J. Abrams

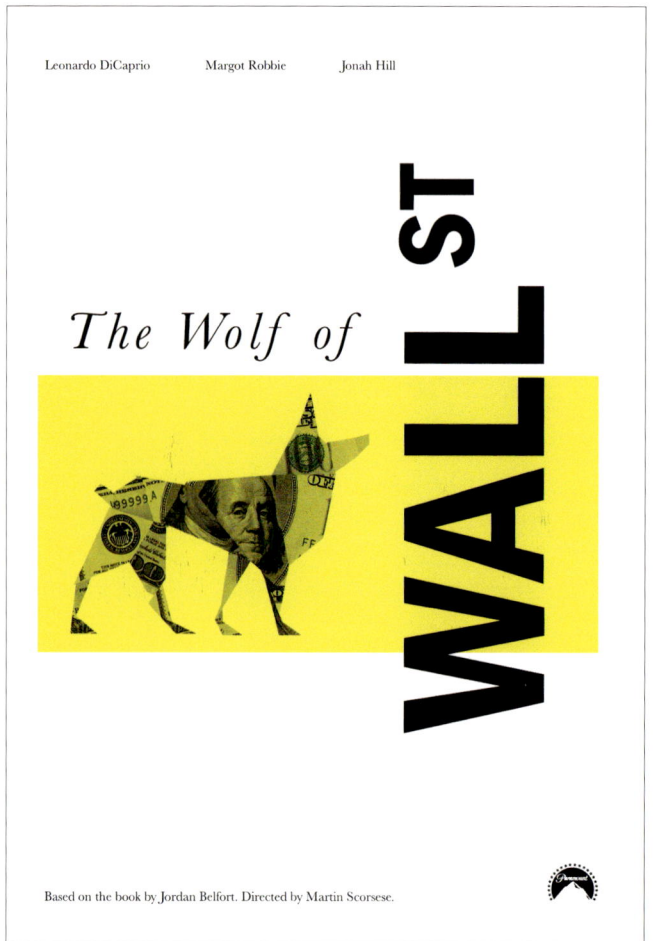

Leonardo DiCaprio   Margot Robbie   Jonah Hill

The Wolf of

WALL ST

Based on the book by Jordan Belfort. Directed by Martin Scorsese.

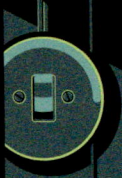

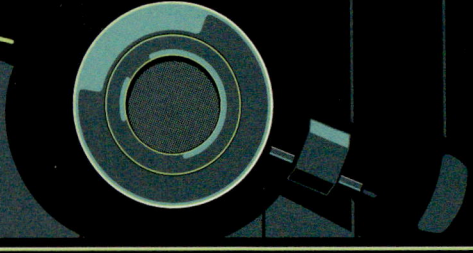

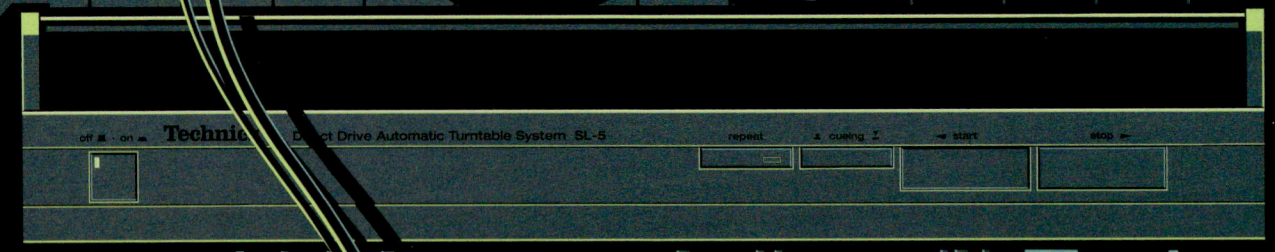

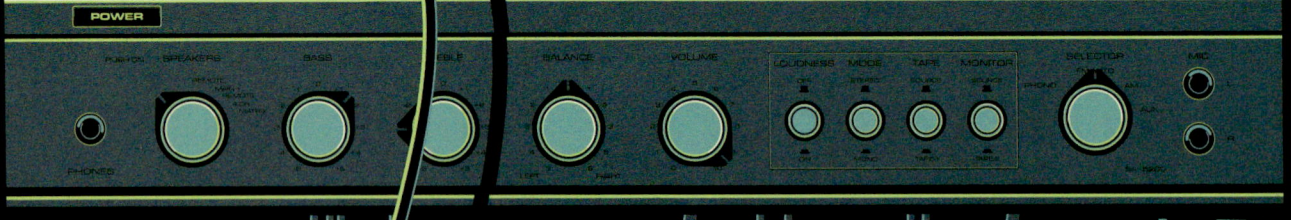

Salvador Anguiano

SALVADOR ANGUIANO
www.be.net/salvador
www.posterspy.com/profile/salvador

I grew up as the son of a working, single mom and spent most of my childhood glued to the TV, from afternoon until pretty late at night. Once I was done watching cartoons and reading comic books, I just watched whatever VHS was laying around the house, which was mostly rom-coms. I was introduced to such '80s classics as *Footloose*, *Breakfast Club*, *Pretty in Pink*, *Some Kind of Wonderful*, and most John Hughes' movies, later I was able to talk my mom into buying me true cinematic gems like *Cobra*, *Terminator*, *Rambo*, *Lethal Weapon*, *RoboCop*, and all that great stuff. I grew up watching and loving movies, so as I grew tired of the graphic design practice, I decided to return to my childhood love and draw cool stuff I saw in the movies. I focus mostly on what made my childhood fun and try to carry that enthusiasm to my daily life. It has been an awesome ride so far.

VI

I AM A JEDI.
LIKE MY FATHER BEFORE ME.

STAR
WARS

MARVEL
AVENGERS
AGE OF ULTRON

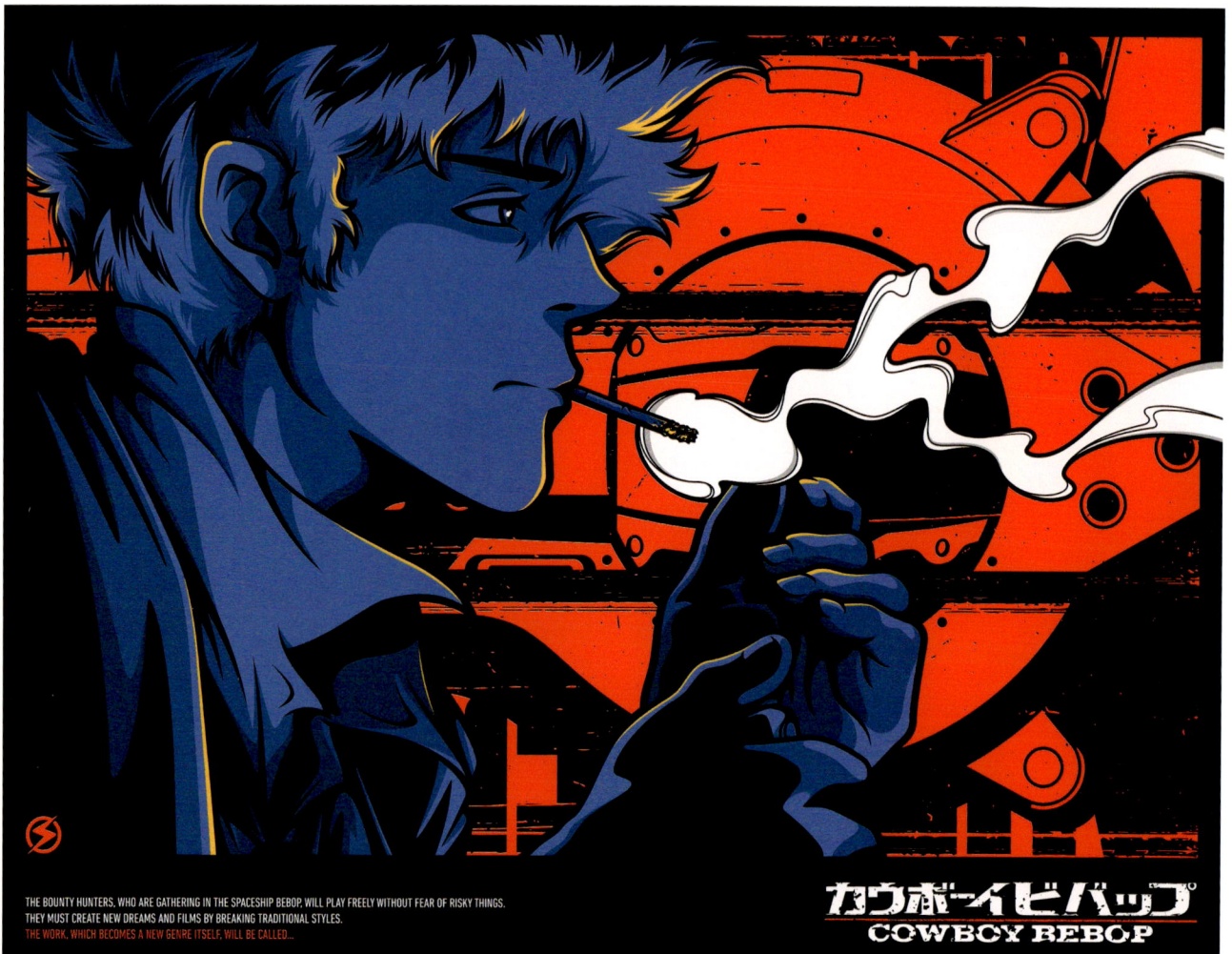

THE BOUNTY HUNTERS, WHO ARE GATHERING IN THE SPACESHIP BEBOP, WILL PLAY FREELY WITHOUT FEAR OF RISKY THINGS.
THEY MUST CREATE NEW DREAMS AND FILMS BY BREAKING TRADITIONAL STYLES.
THE WORK, WHICH BECOMES A NEW GENRE ITSELF, WILL BE CALLED...

カウボーイビバップ
COWBOY BEBOP

PATRICK SWAYZE   KEANU REEVES

POINT BREAK

IT WAS NEVER ABOUT THE MONEY

Salvador Anguiano

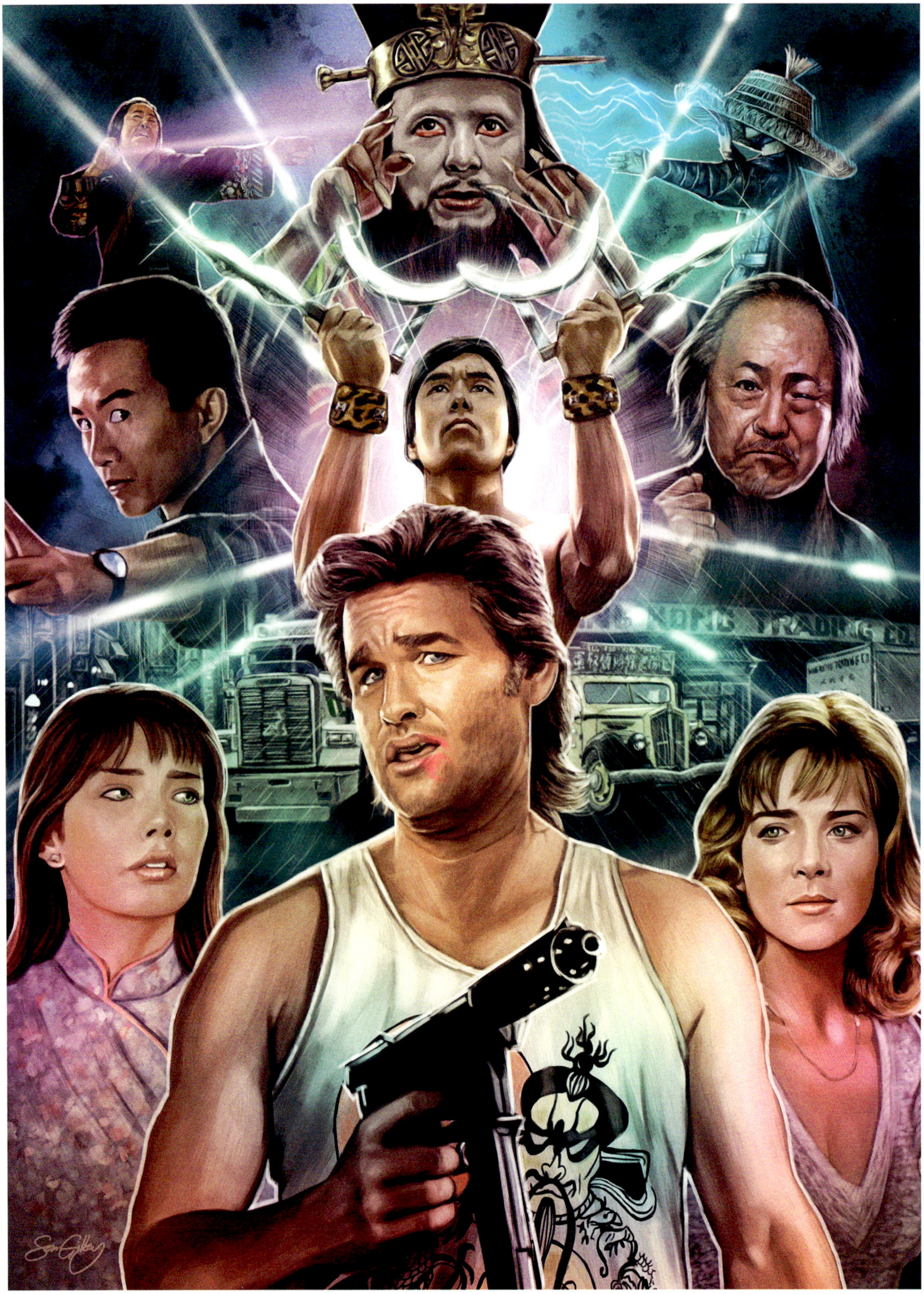

SAM GILBEY
www.samgilbeyillustrates.com
www.posterspy.com/profile/samgilbey

Painted movie posters were really the first kind of art that enthralled me as a child. I remember looking at posters for *Star Wars* in particular, and just being thrilled by the way the various elements combined, the huge characters offset by the tiny action beats, the use of color to accentuate mood, and so on. In fact, it was that excitement that I wanted to channel for myself, and, along with comics, movie posters were really the reason I drew pretty much every day growing up. Many years later, and as a professional artist, I still feel the same way. Whether you think of how to distill a movie down into a single iconic image, or celebrate it by creating a dramatic collage of various characters and elements, it's a puzzle I always love to try and solve, and I can't see myself getting tired of trying anytime soon.

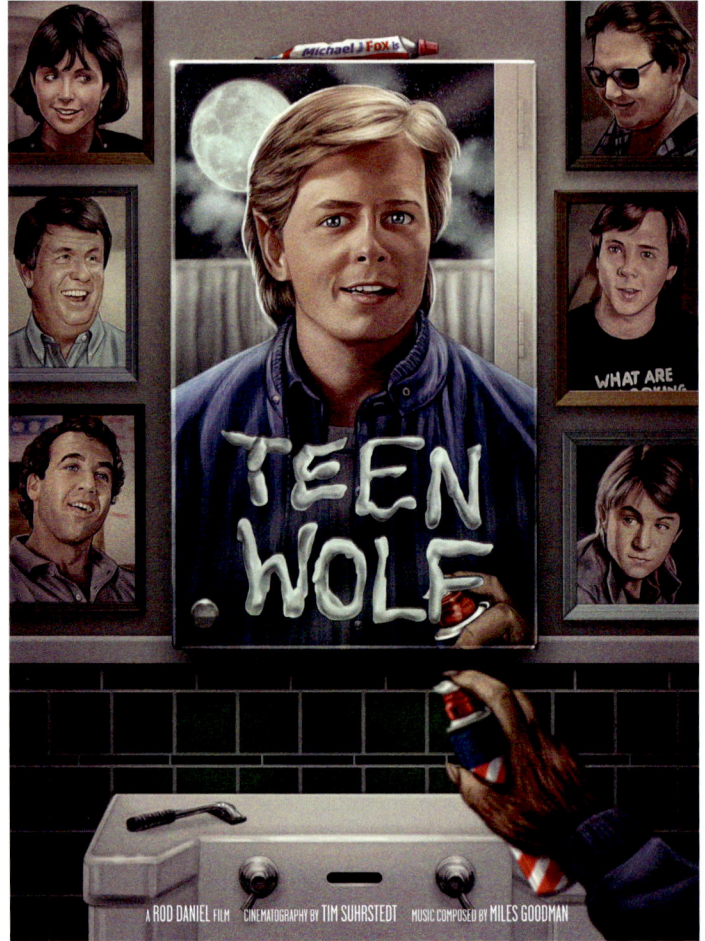

A ROD DANIEL FILM   CINEMATOGRAPHY BY TIM SUHRSTEDT   MUSIC COMPOSED BY MILES GOODMAN

ALFRED HITCHCOCK'S
PSYCHO

A UNIVERSAL RELEASE ALFRED HITCHCOCK'S "PSYCHO" STARRING ANTHONY PERKINS
VERA MILES JOHN GAVIN CO-STARRING MARTIN BALSAM JOHN McINTIRE
AND JANET LEIGH AS MARION CRANE DIRECTED BY ALFRED HITCHCOCK
SCREENPLAY BY JOSEPH STEFANO BASED ON THE NOVEL BY ROBERT BLOCH
© 1960 SHAMLEY PRODUCTIONS, INC. RENEWAL 1988 BY UNIVERSAL STUDIOS.
ALL RIGHTS RESERVED.

SCOTT SASLOW
www.scottsaslow.com
www.posterspy.com/profile/scott_saslow

It was a couple years after graduating film school that I realized filmmaking might not be for me after all. Graphic design had always been the other thing I was interested in and some time after turning twenty-nine, I realized, "I need to go back to school! I can't be a temp forever!" So back to school I went: Florida Atlantic University (magna cum laude '15). I was one of maybe two or three students who infused their work with any kind of pop culture influence and I soon realized that the ultimate goal was to combine both interests: film/TV and graphic design. After quitting my first post-school design job, I read about a designer who was doing one movie poster a day. I was in a funk and naturally I thought, "Why not me?" I enjoy the challenge of creating a singular image that needs to encapsulate an entire narrative —the simpler the better (wittier is best!). My heroes are guys like Brandon Schaefer, Peter Mendelsund, Neil Kellerhouse, and Adam Juresko—designers who favor photographic over purely illustrative solutions. In any case, it's been a fun ride and I've encountered all sorts of wonderful and creative people!

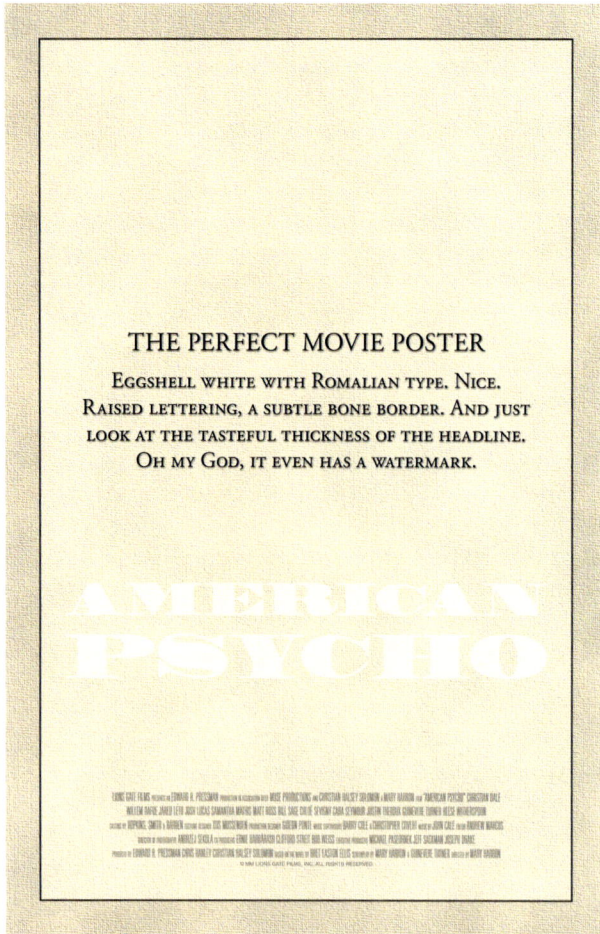

AMERICAN PSYCHO

THE PERFECT MOVIE POSTER

Eggshell white with Romalian type. Nice. Raised lettering, a subtle bone border. And just look at the tasteful thickness of the headline. Oh my God, it even has a watermark.

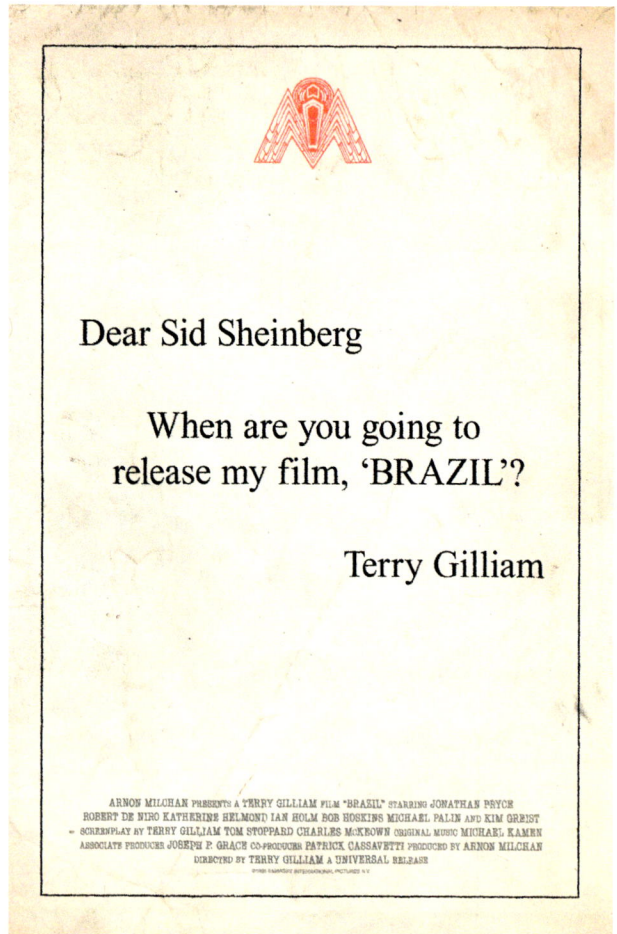

Dear Sid Sheinberg

When are you going to release my film, 'BRAZIL'?

Terry Gilliam

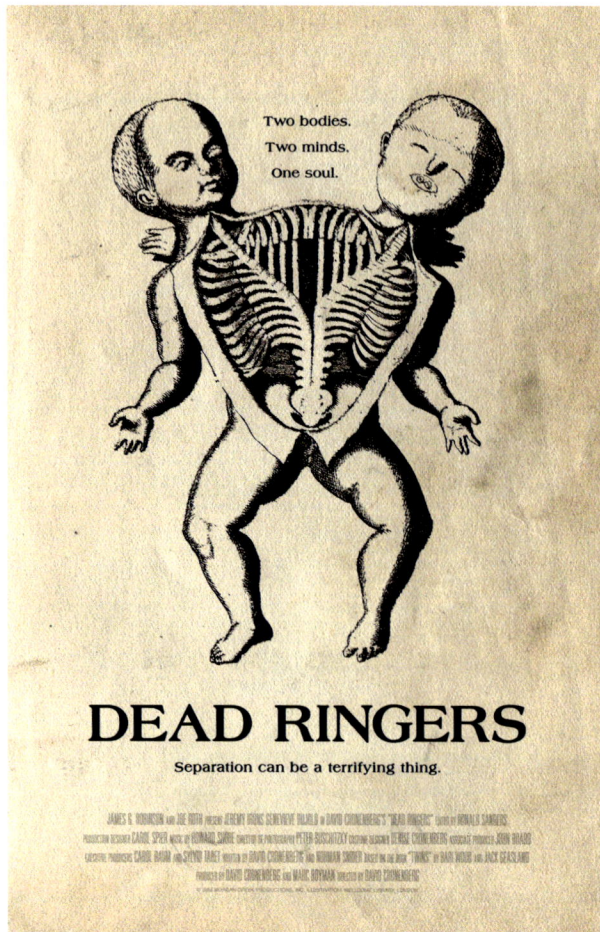

Two bodies.
Two minds.
One soul.

DEAD RINGERS

Separation can be a terrifying thing.

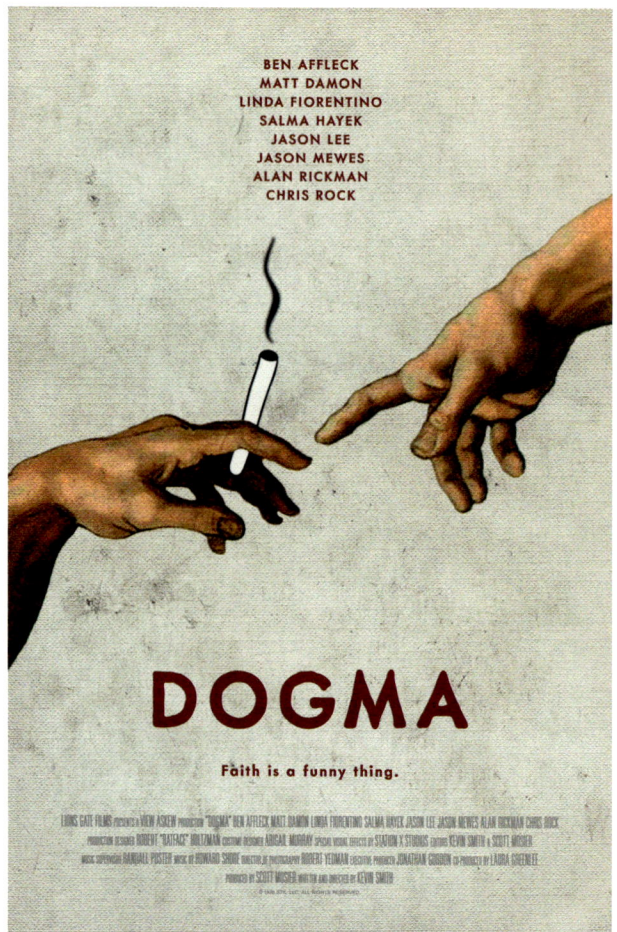

BEN AFFLECK
MATT DAMON
LINDA FIORENTINO
SALMA HAYEK
JASON LEE
JASON MEWES
ALAN RICKMAN
CHRIS ROCK

DOGMA

Faith is a funny thing.

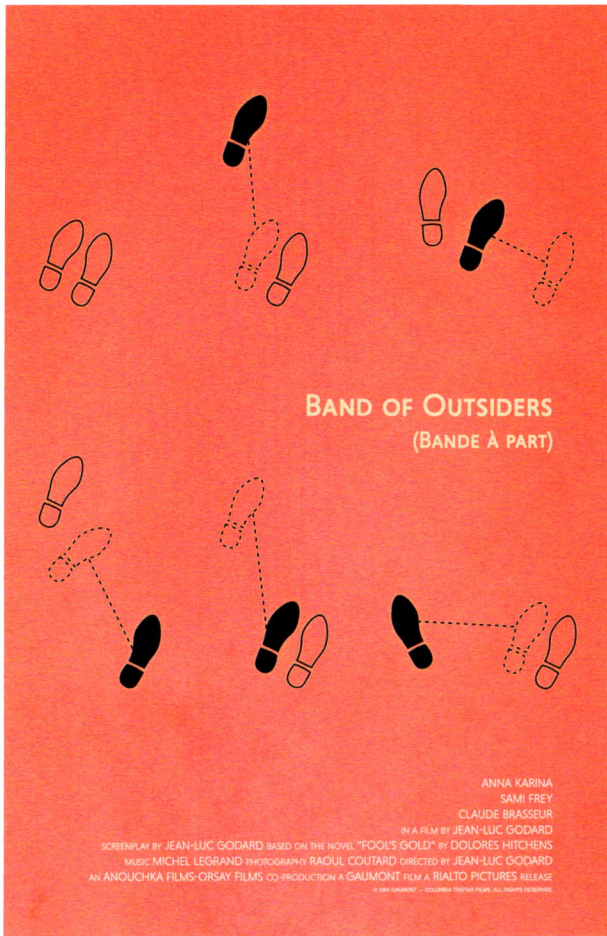

BAND of OUTSIDERS
(Bande à part)

ANNA KARINA
SAMI FREY
CLAUDE BRASSEUR
in a film by JEAN-LUC GODARD
SCREENPLAY BY JEAN-LUC GODARD BASED ON THE NOVEL "FOOL'S GOLD" BY DOLORES HITCHENS
MUSIC MICHEL LEGRAND PHOTOGRAPHY RAOUL COUTARD DIRECTED BY JEAN-LUC GODARD
AN ANOUCHKA FILMS-ORSAY FILMS CO-PRODUCTION A GAUMONT film a RIALTO PICTURES RELEASE
© 1964 GAUMONT — COLUMBIA TRISTAR FILMS. ALL RIGHTS RESERVED.

THERE WILL BE BLOOD

PARAMOUNT VINTAGE AND MIRAMAX FILMS PRESENT JOANNE SELLAR/GHOULARDI FILM COMPANY PRODUCTION DANIEL DAY-LEWIS "THERE WILL BE BLOOD" PAUL DANO KEVIN J. O'CONNOR
CIARÁN HINDS DILLON FREASIER CASTING CINDY TOLAN MUSIC BY JONNY GREENWOOD COSTUME DESIGNER MARK BRIDGES EDITOR DYLAN TICHENOR, A.C.E.
DIRECTOR OF PHOTOGRAPHY ROBERT ELSWIT CO-PRODUCER ERIC SCHLOSSER EXECUTIVE PRODUCER SCOTT RUDIN PRODUCTION DESIGNER DAVID WILLIAMS PRODUCED BY JOANNE SELLAR PAUL THOMAS ANDERSON DANIEL LUPI
BASED ON THE NOVEL "OIL!" BY UPTON SINCLAIR SCREENPLAY WRITTEN AND DIRECTED BY PAUL THOMAS ANDERSON
™ & COPYRIGHT © 2007 BY PARAMOUNT VANTAGE, A DIVISION OF PARAMOUNT PICTURES. ALL RIGHTS RESERVED.

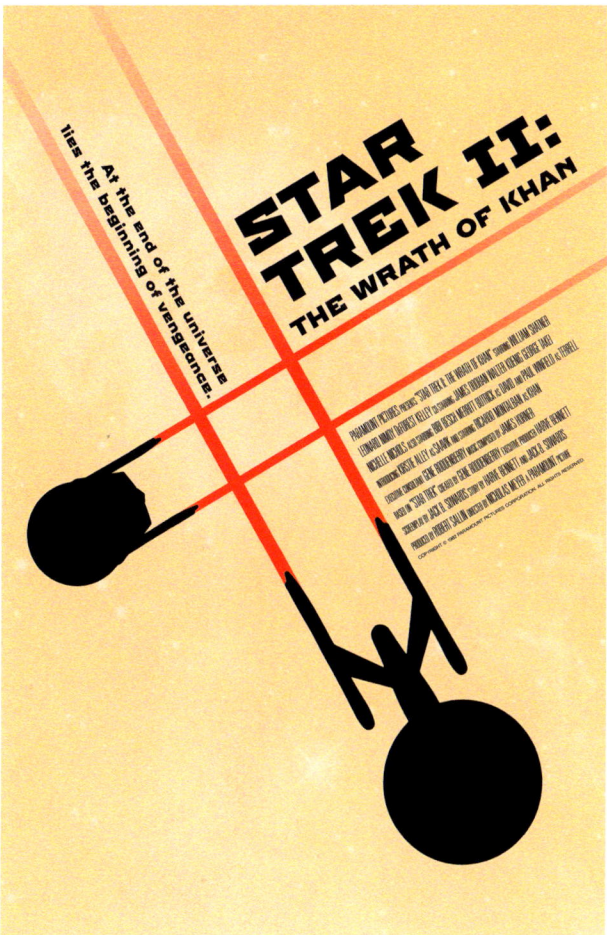

At the end of the universe
lies the beginning of vengeance.

STAR TREK II:
THE WRATH OF KHAN

PARAMOUNT PICTURES PRESENTS "STAR TREK II: THE WRATH OF KHAN" STARRING WILLIAM SHATNER
LEONARD NIMOY DeFOREST KELLEY CO-STARRING JAMES DOOHAN WALTER KOENIG GEORGE TAKEI
NICHELLE NICHOLS ALSO STARRING BIBI BESCH MERRITT BUTRICK AND INTRODUCING PAUL WINFIELD AS TERRELL
KIRSTIE ALLEY AS SAAVIK MUSIC COMPOSED BY JAMES HORNER
EXECUTIVE CONSULTANT GENE RODDENBERRY BASED UPON "STAR TREK" CREATED BY GENE RODDENBERRY
STORY BY HARVE BENNETT AND JACK B. SOWARDS
SCREENPLAY BY JACK B. SOWARDS PRODUCED BY ROBERT SALLIN DIRECTED BY NICHOLAS MEYER A PARAMOUNT PICTURE
COPYRIGHT © 1982 PARAMOUNT PICTURES CORPORATION. ALL RIGHTS RESERVED.

Steve Martin   John Candy   A John Hughes Film

PLANES, TRAINS AND AUTOMOBILES

PARAMOUNT PICTURES Presents A JOHN HUGHES Film STEVE MARTIN JOHN CANDY
PLANES, TRAINS AND AUTOMOBILES Music Score by IRA NEWBORN Edited by PAUL HIRSCH
Director of Photography DON PETERMAN, A.S.C. Executive Producers MICHAEL CHINICH and NEIL MACHLIS
Written, Produced and Directed by JOHN HUGHES A PARAMOUNT Picture
™ & COPYRIGHT © 1987 BY PARAMOUNT PICTURES CORPORATION. ALL RIGHTS RESERVED.

SG POSTERS (EILEEN STEINBACH)
www.sg-posters.com
www.posterspy.com/profile/sg

I've been a fan of movies my whole life and the creativity and hard work that goes into them—from writing to production, cinematography, and costumes. All the pieces that together create something that lets you forget about the world for a bit and dive into the story. Movie posters are the door to the outside for me, luring the viewer in, catching attention. And a few years ago, it became a hobby of mine to create alternative versions of the movie posters I love, a different approach to the mainstream designs, intriguing yet simple. I'm a minimalist at heart, and I try to create imagery representative of the film but also that gets to the core: iconic or visually interesting pieces in different styles but always with my very own personal signature. It's a great way to let my mind run free apart from my day job as a graphic designer and I'm grateful I found this truly inspiring community of designers and illustrators to unite my passion for movies and design that opened so many doors already.

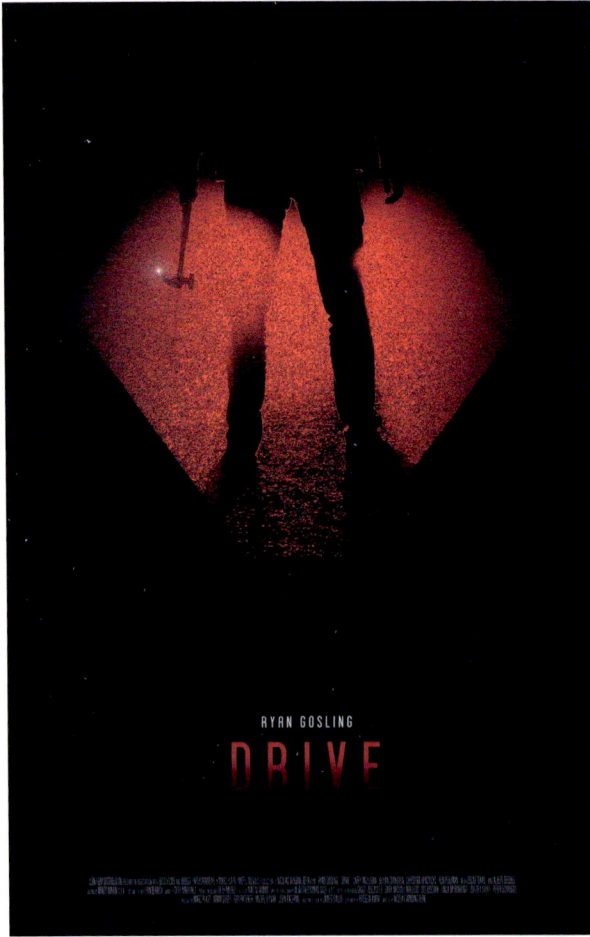

RYAN GOSLING
DRIVE

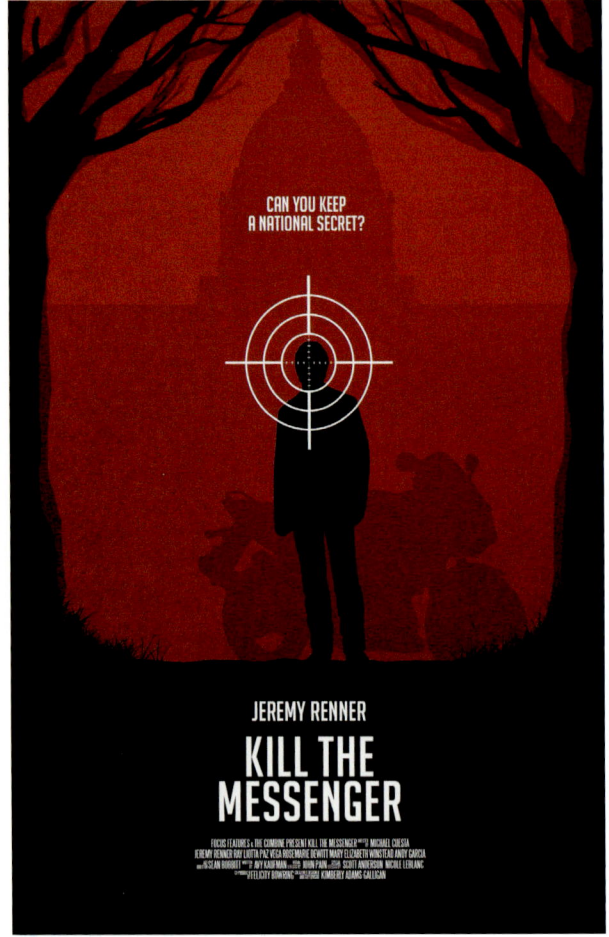

CAN YOU KEEP
A NATIONAL SECRET?

JEREMY RENNER
KILL THE
MESSENGER

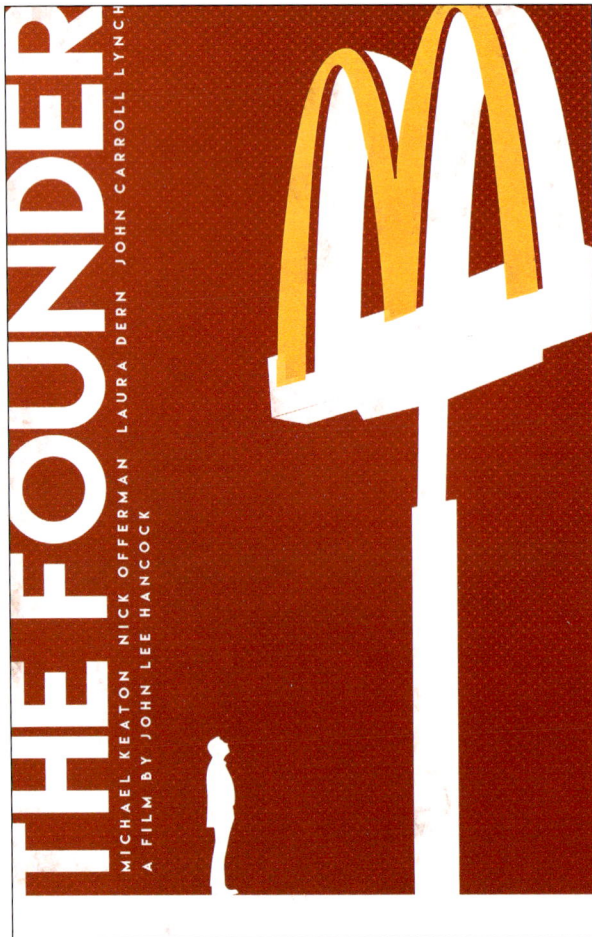

THE FOUNDER

MICHAEL KEATON NICK OFFERMAN LAURA DERN JOHN CARROLL LYNCH
A FILM BY JOHN LEE HANCOCK

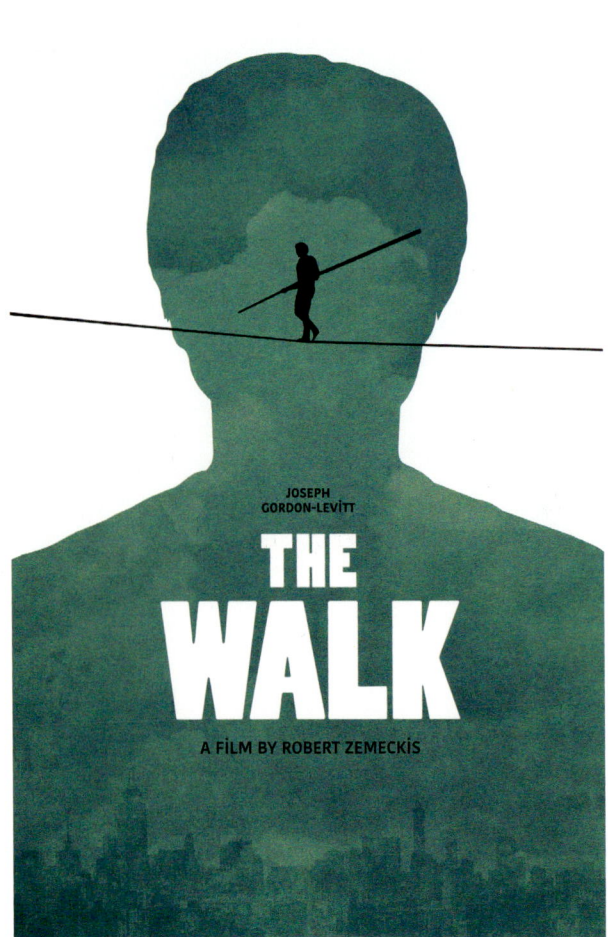

JOSEPH
GORDON-LEVITT
THE
WALK
A FILM BY ROBERT ZEMECKIS

Crimson Peak

LEGENDARY PICTURES and UNIVERSAL PICTURES present A LEGENDARY PICTURES / DDY PRODUCTION A GUILLERMO DEL TORO FILM CRIMSON PEAK MIA WASIKOWSKA JESSICA CHASTAIN
TOM HIDDLESTON CHARLIE HUNNAM and JIM BEAVER MUSIC FERNANDO VELÁZQUEZ COSTUME KATE HAWLEY EDITED BERNAT VILAPLANA PRODUCTION TOM SANDERS PHOTOGRAPHY DAN LAUSTSEN
EXECUTIVE JILLIAN SHARE PRODUCERS THOMAS TULL JON JASHNI AND GUILLERMO DEL TORO PRODUCED CALLUM GREENE WRITTEN GUILLERMO DEL TORO & MATTHEW ROBBINS DIRECTED GUILLERMO DEL TORO

SIMON CARPENTER
www.simonthegreat.co.uk
www.posterspy.com/profile/simonthegreat

For as long as I can remember, I have quite simply loved films and REALLY LOVED drawing. My earliest memories are of sketching the Ghostbusters and He-Man in "stick man" form (hopefully my skills have improved a bit since then). I have always been a creative person and it seemed only natural to combine my two passions into the production of art based on some of my favorite films.

The art of the film poster has evolved so much and I've tried to develop a style that combines the traditional with a modern approach. Most of my art is painted digitally on a graphics tablet with some effects added in Photoshop afterwards. My biggest artistic inspirations would have to be Drew Struzan, as well as Jock and Francesco Francavilla. Although the latter two may be better known as comic artists, their poster artwork really speaks to me and makes me strive to improve my own work.

I much prefer posters with intelligent, striking design rather than a few simple photos of the stars from whatever film it is. The artists that produce work for Mondo are a prime example of this and how illustrated film posters can still be exciting and interesting. It really is an honor to be included in this book with so many talented artists and I hope you enjoy my art as much as I enjoy creating it.

THE
NEON
DEMON
THE NEW FILM BY
NICOLAS WINDING REFN

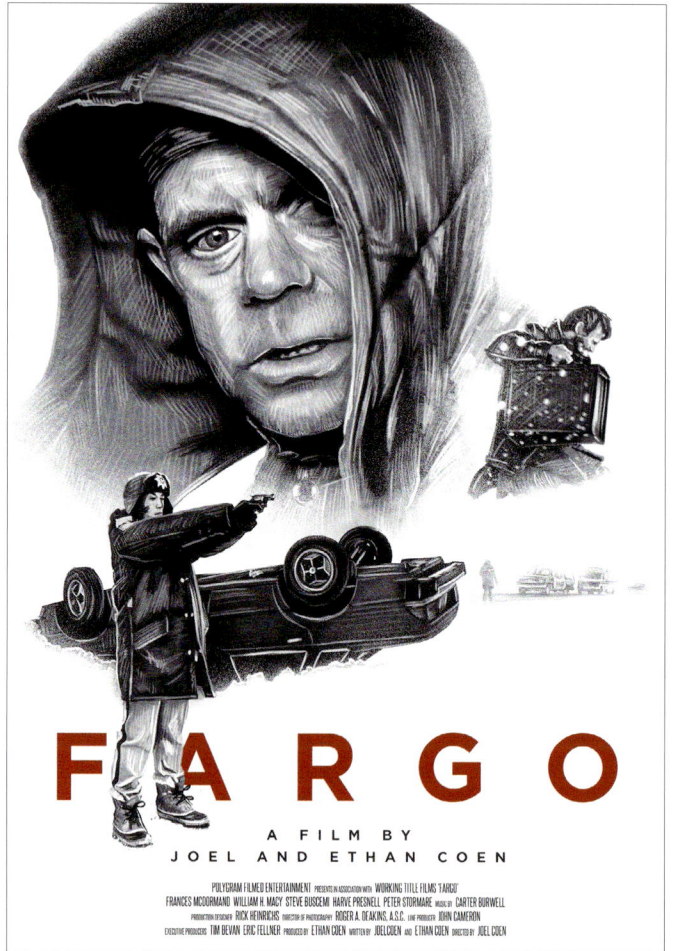

F A R G O

A FILM BY
JOEL AND ETHAN COEN

POLYGRAM FILMED ENTERTAINMENT PRESENTS IN ASSOCIATION WITH WORKING TITLE FILMS 'FARGO'
FRANCES McDORMAND WILLIAM H. MACY STEVE BUSCEMI HARVE PRESNELL PETER STORMARE MUSIC BY CARTER BURWELL
PRODUCTION DESIGNER RICK HEINRICHS DIRECTOR OF PHOTOGRAPHY ROGER A. DEAKINS, A.S.C. LINE PRODUCER JOHN CAMERON
EXECUTIVE PRODUCERS TIM BEVAN ERIC FELLNER PRODUCED BY ETHAN COEN WRITTEN BY JOEL COEN and ETHAN COEN DIRECTED BY JOEL COEN

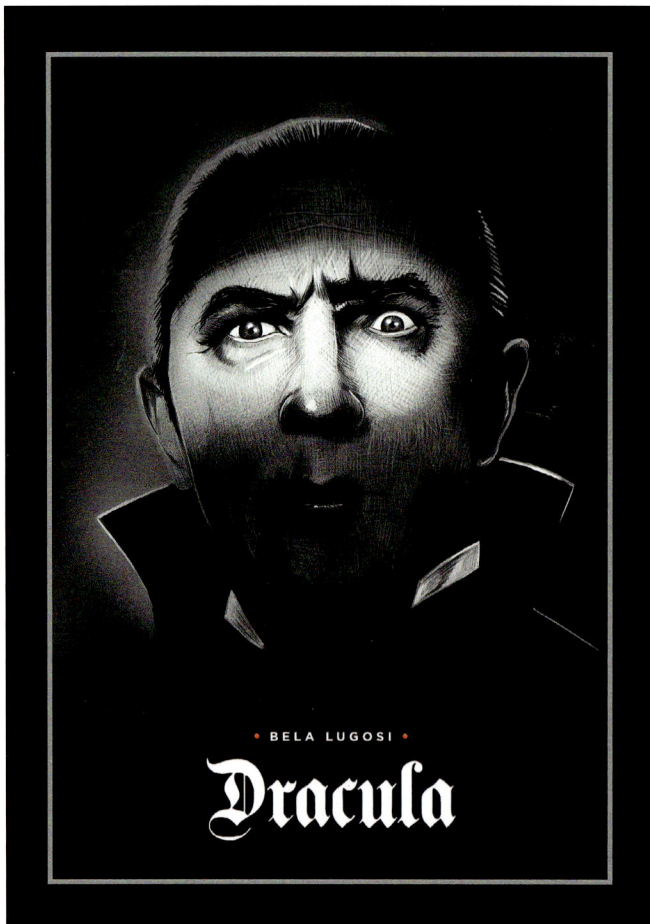

· BELA LUGOSI ·
Dracula

GEORGE A. ROMERO'S
DAY
OF THE
DEAD

SIMON CARUSO
www.simoncaruso.com
www.posterspy.com/profile/simon-caruso

For a few years, we've seen artists from all over the world taking ownership of the commonly called geek/pop culture. Our generation grew up watching awesome movies (thank you Mr. Spielberg and Co.), and today we love to pay homage to these fantastic storytellers and spread this influence to the next generations!

I love how each artist works on what he loves and submits his personal vision of one movie, even if we all know its famous official poster; it's a real challenge to create something new! But when art is driven by passion, it's all for the best! I've loved cinema since I was a kid, and a few years ago, as a freelance artist, even if I didn't have a lot of spare time, I wanted to do something personal, and mix together my work and my other passion. Inspired by the works of Scott C, Patrick Connan, Ale Giorgini, or Van Orton, I thought, "Hey, I love cinema. Let's have fun on some personal stuff." Since then I've worked on some art shows at Hero Complex Gallery (Los Angeles), one limited edition poster with AlternativeMoviePosters.com, and took part in tributes with the Poster Posse. I don't have time to produce much, but I try to always have clever ideas and new concepts for the several series I'm currently working on.

ack ! ack ! ack ! ack !

ack ! ack !

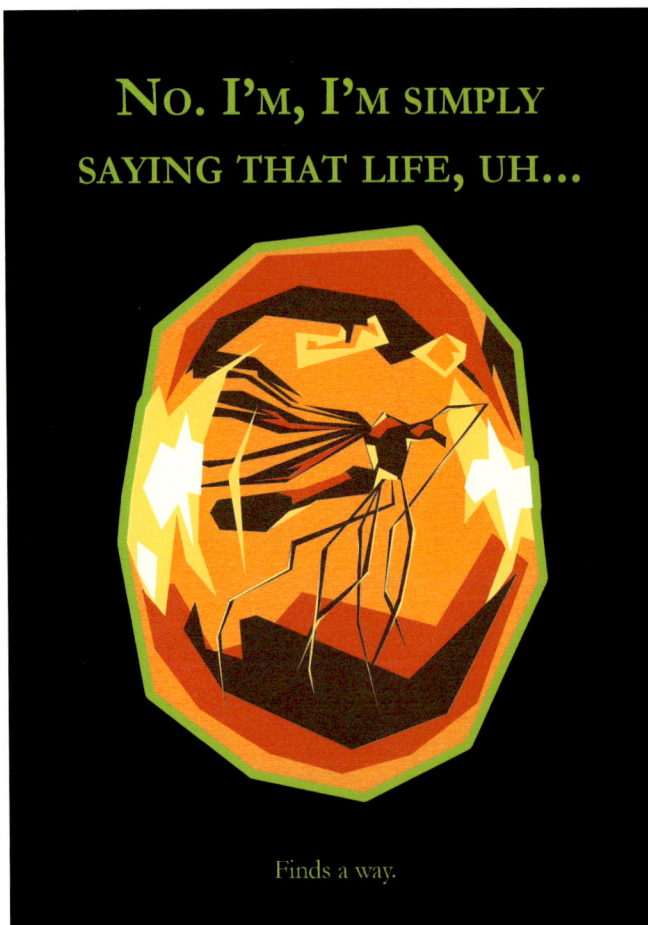

No. I'm, I'm simply saying that life, uh...

Finds a way.

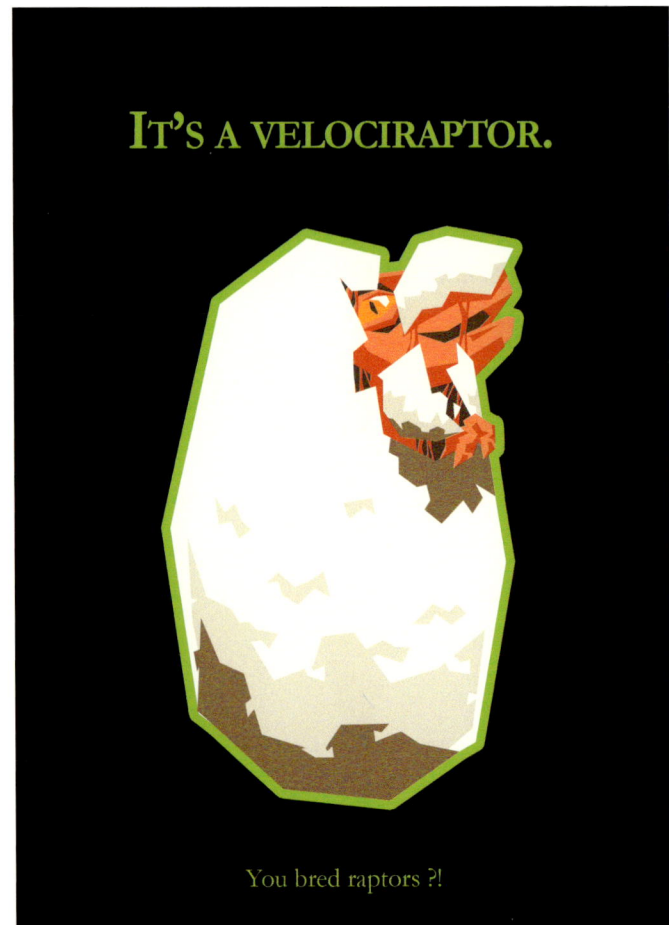

It's a velociraptor.

You bred raptors ?!

SIMON DELART

www.s2lart.com
www.posterspy.com/profile/s2lart

I grew up surrounded by comics, films, and music. My parents had a huge collection of graphic novels and Franco-Belgian comics! They also had a re-edition of the *Fantastic Four* and Kirby's *Silver Surfer*. Comics have been extremely present in my life indeed. In this respect, I must also mention several revelations I had around the time my father recorded Tim Burton's *Batman* for me. First, the film terrified me and fascinated me at the same time. Soon after I unearthed *Strange* magazine volumes at my grandparents' place. Finally, I was influenced by the arrival of *Batman: The Animated Series*. There was also a video club next door. I went there every Wednesday afternoon and

I challenged myself to watch the complete filmography of my idols of that time: Stallone, Van Damme, Shwarzy, Chan, Gibson, etc., etc. All that, sprinkled with video games and Canal + humor, and you get a good '80s/'90s pop culture product!

I was struck with admiration when I contemplated Drew Struzan's posters, and today, his compositions and his colors are real references for me. My desire of making alternative posters stems from my discovery of Olly Moss' work and his ability to find a concept that goes beyond mere illustrations. This challenge motivates me.

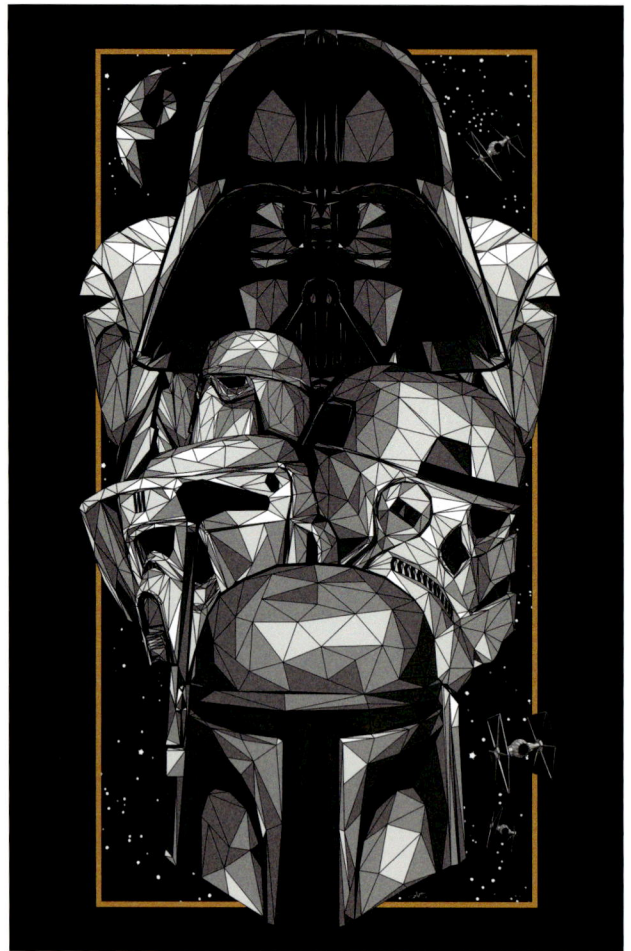

The insect is awake.

THE FLY [18]

A DAVID CRONENBERG FILM Starring JEFF GOLDBLUM • GEENA DAVIS in "THE FLY"
Music by HOWARD SHORE • Screenplay by CHARLES EDWARD POGUE and DAVID CRONENBERG • Produced by STUART CORNFELD • Directed by DAVID CRONENBERG
Prints by DELUXE • Dolby Stereo in Selected Theatres

Much to my house-proud mother's great dismay, my childhood bedroom was absolutely covered with film posters. Every spare inch was a canvas for posters for *Evil Dead II*, *Gremlins*, *Re-Animator*, *The Thing*, *Zombie Flesh Eaters*.... Growing up in the '80s, some of my happiest times were spent wandering the aisles of my local video stores. Surrounded by posters and the often outrageous box art of hundreds of VHS tapes was like visiting the most awesome art gallery imaginable. I'd salvage posters from every video store, local cinema, and corner shop within an hour's bike ride. These things were like treasure and I couldn't get over the fact that they were just going to throw them away. As a full-time designer I'm interested in many aspects of design culture, but nothing gets me quite as excited as movie poster design. It's those iconic images from the past that still inspire me and thousands of other designers and illustrators. The growth of the alternative movie poster scene means that they are producing so much amazing work for no other reason than wanting to share their love and appreciation for the films that mean something special to them. I can't think of any better reason to produce art than that.

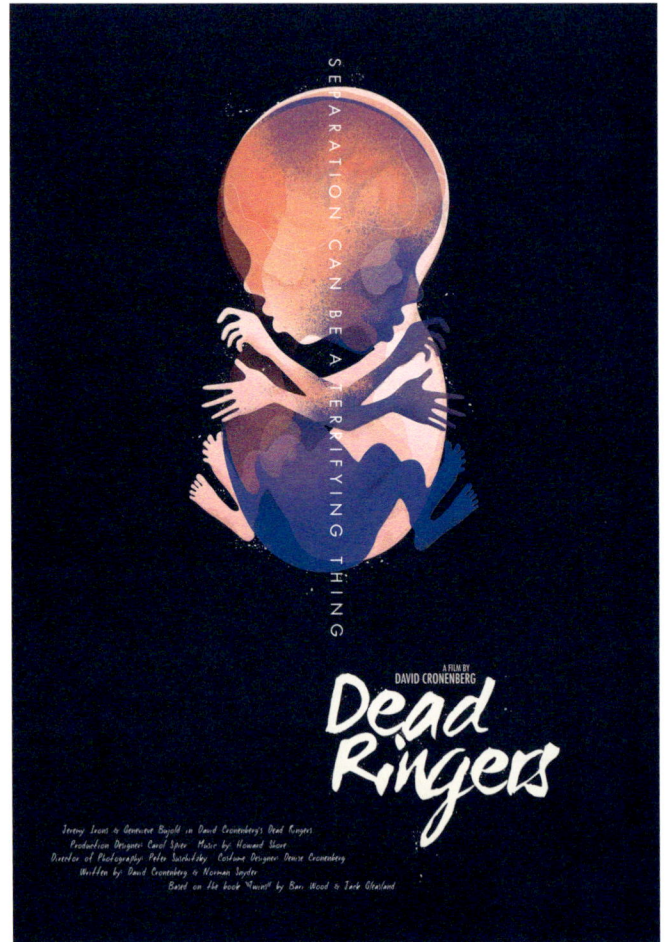

VIDEODROME

PAN'S LABYRINTH

THE DARK INKER (STEPHEN SAMPSON)

www.thedarkinker.com
www.posterspy.com/profile/thedarkinker

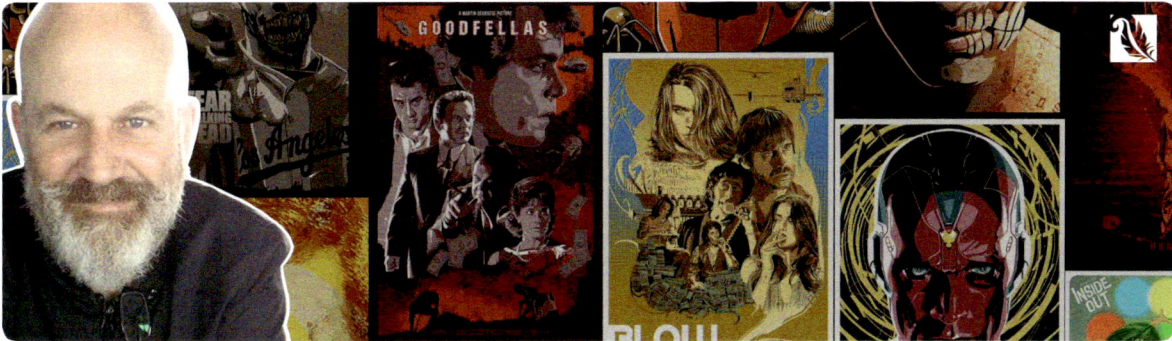

Movies and comics were the two earliest influences on my art. Windows into the imagination and other worlds. Worlds where anything was possible! The movie poster was always the first "look" at what was coming. And the artists that created them were inspirational!

As I've grown older, movies and their posters have played a major part in influencing aspects of my artwork, and it's always a massive blast to create artwork directly connected to some of the world's all-time favorite movies.

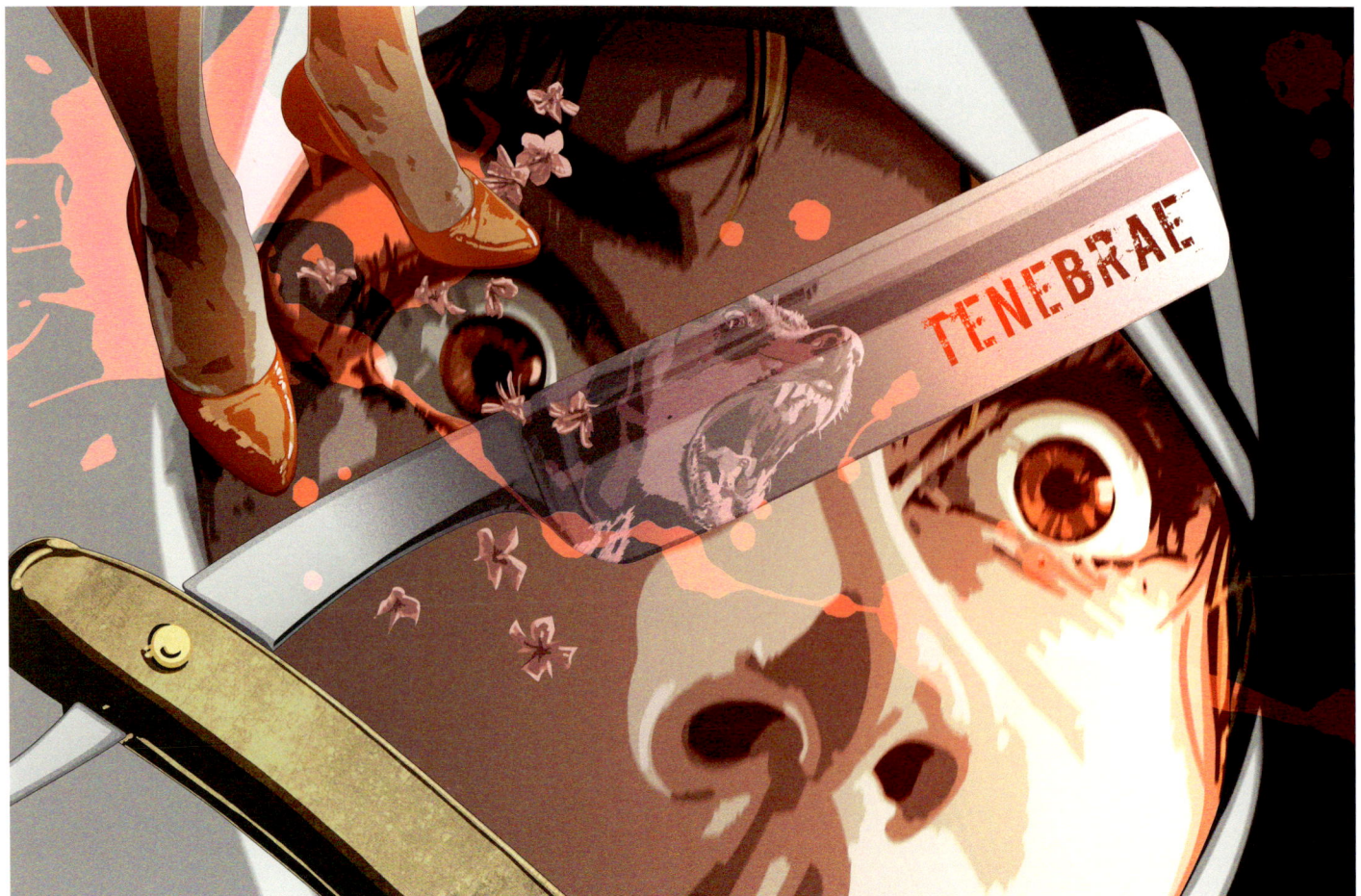

America was born in the streets"

GANGS OF NEW YORK

LEONARDO DICAPRIO DANIEL DAY-LEWIS CAMERON DIAZ
A MARTIN SCORSESE PICTURE

STUDIO MURUGIAH
www.studiomurugiah.com
www.posterspy.com/profile/sharm-murugiah

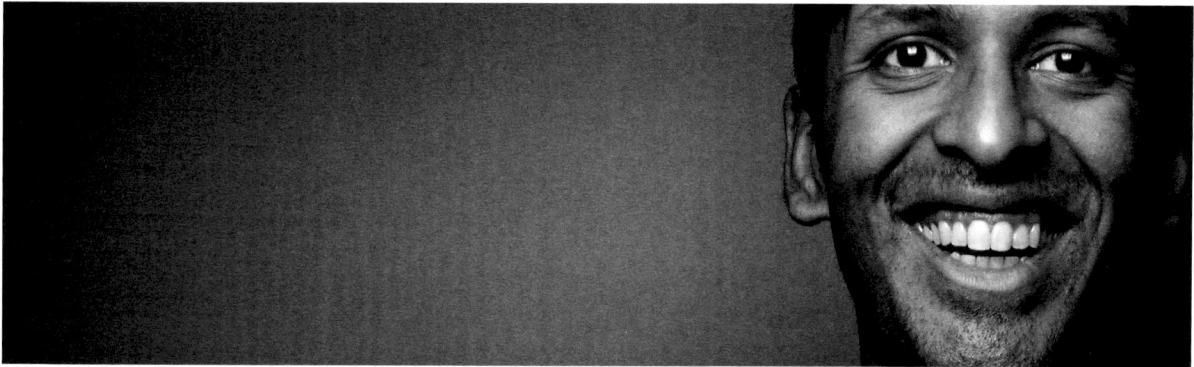

I love movie posters for the simple reason that they are able to capture the essence of a film. Whether you've seen a film poster for a flick that's a few weeks out from its release or you've seen a great flick and you want to preserve that memory as an art print on your wall. Film posters are able to grab you in ways you wouldn't think. Film posters have been around for a very long time. From the beautiful artwork of Saul Bass to Bob Peak right through to Drew Struzan. These artists have made successful careers out of capturing moments in film that fans remember and talk about well after the film has been made. Over the last 10–15 years official movie posters that come from the studios have generally been quite dull Photoshopped floating heads of the stars of the film, photography that has been used without creativity. But we are currently going through a bit of a renaissance in creating beautiful art for film posters. It is, unfortunately been relegated to the area of a "special edition alternative art poster" instead of key art for film advertising, but nevertheless, amazing art is being created. PosterSpy and the rest of the artists in this book are part of that movement. Ultimately we are all fans of film and that's what drives us to create beautiful art!

WORST HEROES EVER
DAVID AYER
2016

30 YEARS AGO
FOUR FRIENDS SAVED THE WORLD
GHOSTBUSTERS
8·HOOK & LADDER·8
THIS SUMMER
A NEW TEAM
WILL ANSWER
THE CALL

a film by
Michel Gondry
Mood Indigo
Based on a novel by
Boris Vian
SACHA BOURDO WITH THE PARTICIPATION OF PHILIPPE TORRETON VINCENT ROTTIERS
LAURENT LAFITTE FROM LA COMEDIE FRANCAISE NATACHA REGNIER ZINEDINE SOUALEM AND ALAIN CHABAT DIRECTED BY MICHEL GONDRY SCREENPLAY BY MICHEL GONDRY AND LUC BOSSI BASED ON THE BOOK BY BORIS VIAN
CINEMATOGRAPHY CHRISTOPHE BEAUCARNE SET DESIGN STÉPHANE ROSENBAUM COSTUMES FLORENCE FONTAINE ORIGINAL MUSIC ÉTIENNE CHARRY EDITING MARIE-CHARLOTTE MOREAU HEAD OF POST PRODUCTION DORIS YOBA
PRODUCTION MANAGER GILLES CASTERA LINE PRODUCER XAVIER CASTANO PRODUCED BY LUC BOSSI A BRIO FILMS STUDIO CANAL FRANCE 2 CINEMA SCOPE PICTURES AND HÉRODIADE COPRODUCTION

TOM FOURNIER

www.tomsdesigns.co.uk
www.posterspy.com/profile/tommo

Stories are one of our most powerful forms of communication. They're not limited to words spoken from one person to another; stories transcend countries, audiences, and generations. They can be told on a page, in movies, song, and art. No matter what age you are, or where in the world you're from, everyone enjoys a good story. That is what I love about film and art to an extent, the chance to completely immerse yourself in the story. I've been designing movie posters for almost a decade and I love it. I'm a huge fan of the greats like Drew Struzan, Bill Gold, and Saul Bass who paved the way for the modernists like Laurent Durieux, Ken Taylor, Tyler Stout, Mike Mitchell, Jock, and your "Average Joe" like me! We all have our own artistic style and we each would have a completely different poster for the same film. That's the beauty of designing movie posters. The story is already there . . . it's how you tell it that sets you apart.

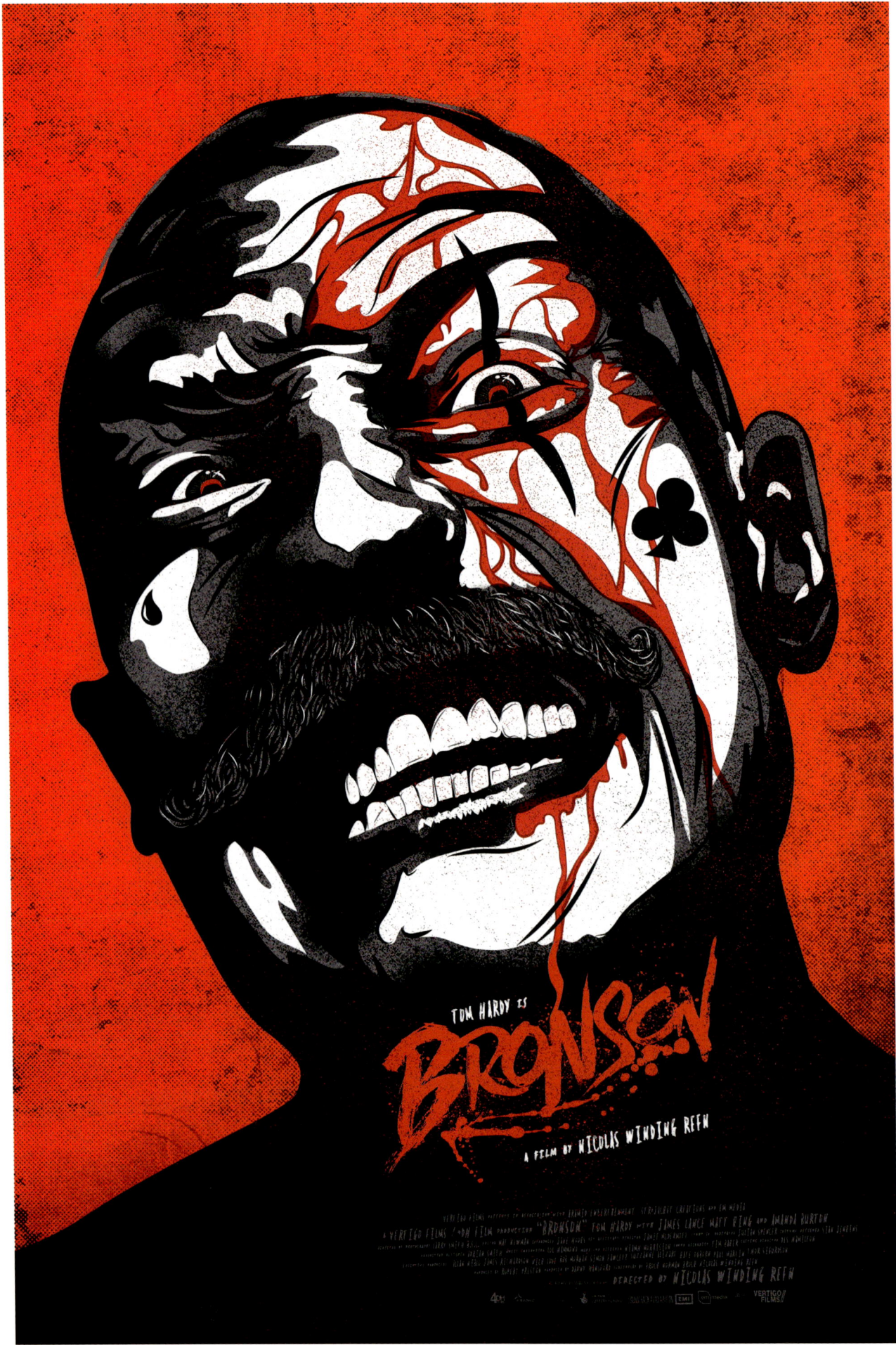

NEO TOKYO IS ABOUT TO
E·X·P·L·O·D·E

ART DIRECTOR TOSHIHARU MIZUTANI
SEQ. SUPERVISOR TAKASHI NAKAMURA
STORY ITO KASHIMOTO
MUSIC SHOJI YAMASHIRO
PRODUCER RYOHEI SUZUKI
CHARACTER DESIGN / SCRIPT / DIRECTOR KATSUHIRO OTOMO
BASED ON THE GRAPHIC NOVEL BY KATSUHIRO OTOMO

TSUCHINOKO
www.tsuchinoko.fr
www.posterspy.com/profile/tsuchinoko

A graphic designer for more than twenty years, Tsuchinoko raged as the art director for French TV Channel M6, has worked with different agencies, and even created his own (10fuze) ten years ago. Nothing escapes his ultra-detailed style with its strong Japanese iconography. His list of partnerships and collaborations is long and includes the worlds of comics (Doggybag) and video games with Konami on MGSV. Tsuchinoko brought his expert touch to a number of different events with live paintings and stencils, as well as a piece on the French National Library that will be talked about for a long time!

GHOST IN THE SHELL

攻殻機動隊

BASED ON THE MANGA BY SHIROW MASAMUNE
DIRECTOR MAMORU OSHII

CHARACTER DESIGN HIROYUKI OKIURA
MECHANICAL DESIGN SHOJI KAWAMORI / ATSUSHI TAKEUCHI
WEAPON DESIGN MITSUO ISO
ART DIRECTOR HIROMASA OGURA
ANIMATION DIRECTOR TOSHIHIKO NISHIKUBO
PRODUCED BY KODANSHA
IN ASSOCIATION WITH
BANDAI VISUAL AND MANGA ENTERTAINMENT
PRODUCTION STUDIO I.G

MUSIC KENJI KAWAI
POSTER DESIGN TSUCHINOKO

234

DJANGO UNCHAINED

a film by QUENTIN TARANTINO

VIKTOR ~ HERTZ

VIKTOR HERTZ
www.viktorhertz.com
www.posterspy.com/profile/hertzen

I've always been a huge fan of movies, but I never thought I'd end up as a graphic designer. In 2010, I started playing around in Illustrator, remixing famous logos and just having fun. Eventually, I made a project called Pictogram movie posters, where I depicted different films using simple pictograms, and apparently it was appreciated online and featured in books and magazines. It was a great way to combine my passion for film and my new fascination for graphics, and it really inspired me to make more posters and it also developed my own style as a graphic designer. It also got me my first freelance jobs, and I still get requests based on my pictogram niche. I really love the process of picking a great film and figuring out how to summarize it's theme and content in my own personal expression. It's a nice combination of paying tribute to my idols and challenging my brain to come up with the best and most clever way to visualize something complex in the simplest way.

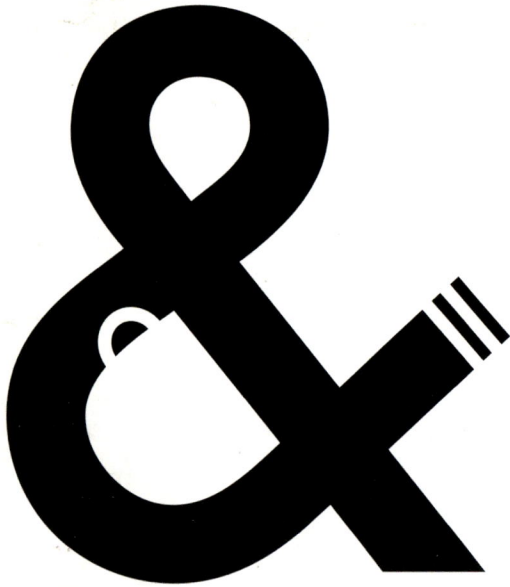

Coffee and cigarettes

A film by Jim Jarmusch

Starring Roberto Benigni, Steven Wright, Joie Lee, Cinqué Lee, Steve Buscemi, Iggy Pop, Tom Waits, Joe Rigano, Vinny Vella, Vinny Vella JR., Renée French, E.J. Rodriguez, Alex Descas, Isaach de Bankolé, Cate Blanchett, Meg White, Jack White, Alfred Molina, Steve Coogan, GZA, RZA, Bill Murray, Bill Rice, Taylor Mead

Rosemary's Baby

A film by Roman Polanski

Starring Mia Farrow John Cassavetes Ruth Gordon Sidney Blackmer Maurice Evans Ralph Bellamy

Up in the air

A film by Jason Reitman

Starring George Clooney Vera Farmiga Anna Kendrick Jason Bateman Amy Morton Melanie Lynskey

Psycho

A film by Alfred Hitchcock

Starring Anthony Perkins Vera Miles John Gavin Janet Leigh Martin Balsam John McIntire

a clockwork orange

a film by **stanley kubrick**

starring **malcolm mcdowell patrick magee michael bates warren clarke**
james marcus michael tarn godfrey quigley michael gover

the big lebowski

a film by **the coen brothers**

starring **jeff bridges john goodman julianne moore steve buscemi**
david huddleston philip seymour hoffman tara reid

Arttitude

POSTERSPY

Frédéric would like to thank: My mom, Caroline; the whole ARTtitude collective and close friends (you know who you are); all the partners we had in the recent ARTtitude history: Blizzard Entertainment, Konami, Bethesda, Focus Home Interactive, Paris Games Week, Elephant Films, The Jokers . . . . This book is dedicated to Baptiste.

Jack would like to thank: My mother, father, family, and friends who always supported me and my passion to create. Most importantly thanks to Ciprian, my friend and PosterSpy's web developer. Without your hard work the PosterSpy website wouldn't even exist, here's to you, buddy.

Follow us on:

- ARTtitude
- arttitude_official
- @FredCLAQUIN
- www.therealarttitude.com

- PosterSpy
- posterspy
- @PosterSpy
- www.posterspy.com

Other Schiffer Books by the Author:

ARTtitude, by Frédéric Claquin, 978-0-7643-4628-6
ARTtitude 2, by Frédéric Claquin, 978-0-7643-4795-5

Other Schiffer Books on Related Subjects:

Alternative Movie Posters: Film Art from the Underground, by Matthew Chojnacki, 978-0-7643-4566-1
Alternative Movie Posters II: More Film Art from the Underground, by Matthew Chojnacki, 978-0-7643-4986-7

Copyright © 2018 by Plan9 Entertainment

Library of Congress Control Number: 2017951907

Cover Artwork: CRANIODSGN
Cover Design: Justin Watkinson
Credits: All the works presented in this book as well as the profile photos belong to the artists who created and/or supplied them. Photograph of Jack Woodhams © Wil Barker 2016.

This book features fifty-eight incredible artists from the PosterSpy art community, visit www.posterspy.com and discover more great poster design.

Type set in Avenir LT Std

ISBN: 978-0-7643-5475-5
Printed in China

Published by Schiffer Publishing, Ltd.
4880 Lower Valley Road
Atglen, PA 19310
Phone: (610) 593-1777; Fax: (610) 593-2002
E-mail: Info@schifferbooks.com
Web: www.schifferbooks.com

For our complete selection of fine books on this and related subjects, please visit our website at www.schifferbooks.com. You may also write for a free catalog.

Schiffer Publishing's titles are available at special discounts for bulk purchases for sales promotions or premiums. Special editions, including personalized covers, corporate imprints, and excerpts, can be created in large quantities for special needs. For more information, contact the publisher.

We are always looking for people to write books on new and related subjects. If you have an idea for a book, please contact us at proposals@schifferbooks.com.

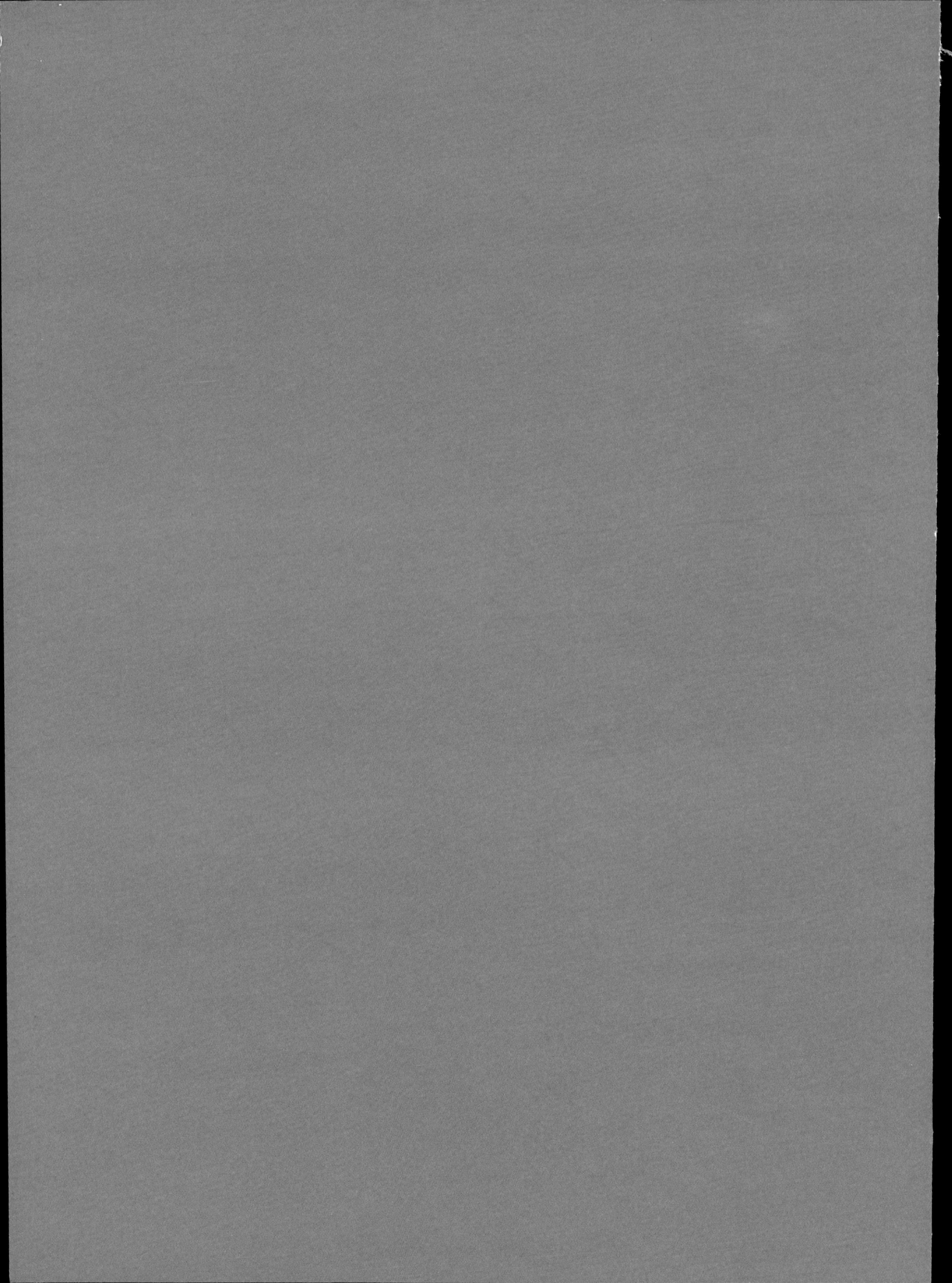